Sea/History   #1473

Building Early American
WARSHIPS

The Journal of the **Rhode Island** *Committee*
for Constructing the Continental Frigates
Providence &   Warren *1775-1777*

Introduction, Illustrations & Plans by
JOHN FITZHUGH MILLAR

LIBRARY OF CONGRESS
Library of Congress Cataloging-in-Publication Data

Building early American warships : the journal of the Rhode Island
committee for constructing the Continental frigates Providence &
Warren, 1775-1777 / introduction, illustrations & plans by John
Fitzhugh Millar.
      p.   cm.
  Bibliography: p.
  Includes index.
  ISBN 0-934943-14-1 (lib. bdg. : alk. paper) : $16.00.   ISBN
0-934943-13-3 (pbk. : alk. paper) : $10.00
    1. Providence (Ship : Launched 1776) 2. Warren (Ship) 3. United
States. Continental Navy--History. 4. United States. Continental
Navy--Boats. 5. Shipbuilding--United States--History--18th century.
6. United States--History--Revolution, 1775-1783--Engineering and
construction.   I. Millar, John Fitzhugh.
E273.P75B84 1988
973.3'5--dc19   Published jointly by   88-8561
                                                                   CIP

Thirteen Colonies Press   Rhode Island Publications Society
710 South Henry Street   77 Plain Street
Williamsburg, Virginia 23185   Providence, Rhode Island 02903

Sewn paperback   0-934943-13-3
Hard cover   0-934943-14-1

LC-87-81258

This book is set primarily in Baskerville type. John Baskerville (1706-1775) devised this beautiful type in the 1750s in
England and it remains unexcelled today. Benjamin
Franklin was most enthusiastic about Baskerville's type
designs, but they were not used in the U.S.A. until the end
of the eighteenth century.

DEDICATION

To my father, John Humphrey Millar,
who first taught me to sail when I was
barely old enough to say, "Daddy, it's tipping!"

TABLE OF CONTENTS

ACKNOWLEDGMENTS

In the early 1970s, while I was a member of the Rhode Island Bicentennial Commission, it was decided to publish a series of monographs of original narratives that shed important light on Rhode Island's participation in the War for Independence. The publications would be financed by a sister organization, the Rhode Island Bicentennial Foundation. Unfortunately, money was short for most of the ambitious bicentennial projects, and many of the important monographs have not yet been published. The work of the Rhode Island Bicentennial Foundation has since been taken over by the Rhode Island Publications Society.

Because I had been responsible for the construction of full-sized operational reproductions of the 24-gun frigate *Rose* and the 12-gun Continental sloop *Providence*, I was asked to write an introduction to the journal of the committee for building the Continental frigates *Warren* and *Providence*. So much needed to be said to set the stage for the actual journal that the resulting work somewhat resembles the tail wagging the dog.

The original journal is a prized possession of the Rhode Island Historical Society Library, and I am indebted to the society's director, Albert T. Klyberg, for making the manuscript available for publication and for valuable assistance in the planning of the book. Other members of the Bicentennial Commission were similarly helpful, particularly Professor Patrick Conley of Providence College and Professor Joel Cohen of the University of Rhode Island.

The editing of the manuscript was handled by David Swain, Paul Campbell, and Hilliard Beller, all of whom made useful suggestions for the improvement of my introductory material. Mr. John Sayen, Jr., of Washington, DC has kindly supplied me with obscure references to some of the less well-known ships of the Continental Navy.

Finally, I would like to thank my wife, Cathy, for her patience and support over the years while I was writing and conducting research for this and all my other books.

John Fitzhugh Millar
Williamsburg, Virginia, 1987

INTRODUCTION

From very early times Rhode Islanders were wedded to the sea. Not only does water compose a large part of the area of the state, but the quirks of commercial and political history encouraged the marriage. Two of these quirks that had the most influence were the tiny size of Rhode Island compared to the other colonies and the extraordinarily liberal charter that was granted to Rhode Island.

Under the original charter, by which Rhode Island was one of the only two colonies to elect its governors instead of having crown appointees forced on it, Rhode Island's water-borne commerce thrived. Much of the life in this commerce, however, was the result of smuggling and outright piracy. In fact, these abuses of the liberal charter became so flagrant that towards the end of the seventeenth century Rhode Island became widely known as "Rogues' Island," and as the summer headquarters of the most notorious pirates (who otherwise were based in Jamaica and Hispaniola). Under threat of having the charter withdrawn, the Rhode Island authorities reluctantly let it be known that pirates were no longer welcome. Shortly afterwards, in 1723, twenty-six pirates were hanged at Gravelly Point at the end of Long Wharf in Newport and were buried between the high and low tide marks on Goat Island.

But the smuggling continued with redoubled energy and soon became a way of life. Since most of the power in the colony was in the hands of elected officials, virtually nothing was done to curb the smuggling. Furthermore, while British officials were well aware of the smuggling, they viewed tiny Rhode Island as not worth the trouble of enforcing the customs regulations and concentrated their efforts instead on those centers of trade where royal authority was more secure, such as Boston, New York and Philadelphia.

This British policy of benign neglect was inspired at least in part by Sir Charles Wager, a former Newport boy who had been elevated to First Lord of the British Admiralty. As a result, Newport enriched herself well beyond what would have been expected from the size of the colony. Newport merchants imported goods duty-free from the French, Spanish, Dutch and Danish West Indies and re-exported them to other North American ports; this procedure was both cheaper and quicker for the other North American ports than the legal way, which would have involved importing the goods via Europe.

The most significant imports from the West Indies (chiefly Saint-Domingue and Martinique) were barrels of molasses. The French, hoping to increase sales of brandy in their colonies, had forbidden the manufacture of rum. Therefore, the French West Indies had no use for the large quantity of molasses that was produced as a waste-product in the refining of sugar. Newport merchants were thus able to buy the French molasses at a bargain price, deliver it to Newport and distill it into rum. There were some thirty-nine rum distilleries on the Newport waterfront in the middle of the century, more than all the rest of the distilleries in North America combined.

Some of the rum was shipped to Africa in exchange

for slaves to be shipped to the West Indies in what became known as the Triangle Trade. Some of the rum was used for home consumption. However, the largest part of it was exported to other North American cities, where it was used as a food-preservative. Storing fresh fruit, vegetables, baked goods and even meat in casks of rum kept them fresher for longer periods of time than drying, salting or smoking could do.

By the start of the Seven Years' War with France and Spain in 1756, nearly all of Newport's economy depended in some way on the smuggling of molasses. The economy of the city could have been ruined by the war. Therefore, while an effort was made to earn a living from the war, mostly through outfitting and operating privateers against the enemy, the molasses trade continued to flourish between Newport and the French West Indies via the expediency of a flood of "official" cartel ships for repatriating prisoners of war. The British took note of this flagrant trading with the enemy and vindictively placed new trade restrictions on all the American colonies even before the war had ended.

In taking this action, the British apparently failed to take into account Rhode Island's military expenditures. For example, in the War of Jenkins' Ear (1739–1748) Rhode Island troops and ships contributed materially to the capture of the French fortress at Louisbourg, and Rhode Island merchants outfitted at least twenty ships a year for privateering. During the Seven Years' War, Providence lost almost fifty ships and Newport lost more than a hundred to the French, the Spanish and bad weather.

The British, knowing that customs duties would never be collected in Rhode Island by corrupt officers on shore, sent warships to Newport for that purpose.

The first to arrive was the 8-gun schooner *St. John,* which brought the molasses trade to a temporary halt and angered the citizenry by attempts to "impress" men into her crew and by permitting her crew to steal from the townsfolk with impunity. Governor Stephen Hopkins conferred hurriedly with members of his council, which then voted to order the fort on Goat Island to fire its heavy 18-pounder cannons at the *St. John.* The fort fired thirteen shots, some of which hit the schooner before she could sail away. These were the first shots fired in resistance against British authority in America; the date was July 9, 1764.

The following year, the frigate *Maidstone* arrived to continue the *St. John's* work. An angry Newport mob seized and burned a small schooner that was serving as a tender to the *Maidstone.* In 1769 the British sent the 8-gun sloop *Liberty* to Newport to control the smuggling, and the Newport mob captured her, pillaged her, cut down her spars and cast her adrift; a few hours later she was burned by "persons unknown."

The British reaction to all these incidents was surprisingly mild, and the smuggling continued, bringing great prosperity to Newport merchants. However, in 1772 the British sent still another warship to Rhode Island, the 8-gun schooner *Gaspee.* Her commander, Lieutenant Dudingston, treated Rhode Islanders from the governor on down with undisguised contempt, and he was able to slow down the molasses trade considerably. In June word reached Providence that the *Gaspee* had run aground off Warwick while she was chasing a schooner northward. Before long the hapless *Gaspee* was surrounded by longboats loaded with angry Rhode Islanders, many of them prominent merchants, whose identity was obscured by the darkness. Dudingston was wounded, the crew taken off and the vessel set on fire.

The British were so enraged by this attack on yet another government ship that an official board of enquiry was sent to Newport to look into the incident. In spite of huge rewards, no citizen came forward with information about any of those involved in the burning, so the board was eventually dissolved. The board had been granted the power to indict and send suspects for trial in England, which was a fundamental abridgement of the Rhode Island charter and of British common law. To guard against further British encroachments on the rights of Englishmen living in America, Rhode Island and Virginia reacted to the board of enquiry by leading the other colonies in establishing the committees of correspondence, a significant step on the road to independence.

At the end of 1774 the British sent a larger warship to Newport. The 24-gun frigate *Rose*, under the command of Captain James Wallace, was a formidable adversary. The elimination of the molasses trade by the *Rose* was the chief factor in causing about four-fifths of Newport's population to leave and seek employment elsewhere by October 1775.

Rhode Islanders had no ships that could stand up to Wallace and his reinforcements, so they used the only weapon available to them. They refused to sell him food for the 150 men on the *Rose* and up to 300 men on the other naval vessels that sometimes assisted Wallace. Wallace, in turn, requisitioned food from Rhode Island farms, usually paying for it, but damaging or destroying the farm's buildings if he was given any trouble. He also seized ships that were laden with provisions, not contenting himself with taking only those ships that were smuggling molasses.

On June 12, 1775, the Rhode Island General Assembly created the Rhode Island Navy to recapture some of

the provision ships. This was the first salt-water navy of
any colony in the Revolution and it consisted of two
sloops. Three days later the larger of the two sloops, the
10-gun sloop *Katy* commanded by Abraham Whipple,
recaptured the armed provision sloop *Diana* off James-
town, where she had been used by Wallace to patrol the
channel. In so doing, *Katy* fired the first naval cannon
shots of the Revolution. She was able to retrieve a
number of other prizes that had been taken by Wallace,
but the Rhode Island Navy was clearly not designed to
stand up to the *Rose* herself.

Realising this in August the General Assembly voted
to instruct its delegates in Congress to introduce legislation creating a national navy. Stephen Hopkins intro-
duced at least two bills for that purpose, and the first of
them, as amended by a committee, was passed by
Congress on October 13, 1775. Written into the bill was
authorization to purchase two ships, one of them being,
according to a letter from committee-member Silas
Deane, the Rhode Island sloop *Katy*. The *Katy*, however,
was not immediately available, so Congress passed sup-
plementary legislation authorizing the purchase and
outfitting of a number of merchant ships then at
Philadelphia.

Hopkins, meanwhile, was looking for a Rhode Island
man to serve as commander in chief of the new Navy.
His first choice was Jahleel Brenton of Newport, the
highest-ranking American then serving in the Royal
Navy. When Brenton declined, Hopkins turned to his
own brother Esek, and Congress made the appointment. Now Esek had an unquestioned reputation as a
seaman, but the administration of the Navy proved to
be beyond his abilities. Just over a year after being
appointed, he was suspended and then dismissed from
the service. Although he suffered some personal dis-

grace from his dismissal, Congress realized the shortcomings of the position itself and left it vacant for the
remainder of the war.

In this Navy, besides Esek Hopkins, were a prepon-
derance of Rhode Island officers: Abraham Whipple
and Esek's son John Burroughs Hopkins had participated in the burning of the *Gaspee*; Hoysted Hacker, Sion
Martindale, Joseph Olney, Jack Peck Rathbun, Silas
Talbot and Elisha Warner were all successful Rhode
Island merchant-ship commanders; Stephen Hopkins
himself served as chairman of the Naval Committee in
the Congress until it was replaced in mid-December
1775 by the larger Marine Committee. Also in December two Rhode Island sloops arrived in Philadelphia,
Katy and *Fly*, and they were duly made part of the
Continental Navy; *Katy*, which had been the first vessel
authorized for the Continental Navy three months
previously, was given two additional cannons and had
her name changed to *Providence*.

On December 13, 1775, Congress passed, Stephen
Hopkins' other bill, authorizing the construction from
the keel up of some thirteen frigates varying in size
from 24 to 32 guns:

> The Committee appointed to devise ways and
> means for fitting out a naval armament, brought in
> their report, which being taken into consideration,
> was agreed to as follows:
> That five ships of thirty-two guns, five of twenty-
> eight guns, three of twenty-four guns, making in
> the whole thirteen, can be fitted for the sea proba-
> bly by the last of March next, viz. in New Hamp-
> shire one, in Massachusetts Bay two, in Rhode
> Island two, in Connecticut one, in New York two, in
> Pennsylvania four, and in Maryland one.

   That the cost of these ships so fitted, will not be
more than 66,666 2/3 dollars each, on an average,
allowing two complete suits of sails for each ship,
equal in the whole to 866,666 2/3 dollars.

   That the materials for fitting them may be all
furnished in these colonies, except the articles of
canvas and gun powder; and that therefore it will
be proper the Congress direct the most speedy and
effectual means of importing the said articles of
canvas and powder; that of the former, 7,500
pieces will be wanted, and of the latter, one hundred tons.

   Resolved, That a committee be appointed with full
powers to carry the above report into execution,
with all possible expedition, (except what relates to
canvas and powder) at the expence of the United
Colonies.

   Resolved, That the appointment of the committee
be deferred till to Morrow.

   Resolved, That it be an instruction to the Secret
Committee to embrace the best and earliest oppor-
tunities to procure the quantity of duck and powder in the above report.

   Resolved, That the Committee appointed to fit
out armed vessels, be authorised to give able-
bodied seamen that may be willing to enter on
board the ships of war of the United Colonies, eight
dollars per calendar month.

   This was a much more positive step than merely
taking over and fitting out former merchant vessels
such as the sloop *Katy* and converting them into makeshift warships. Still, these frigates would be severely
limited in their scope: they could be used for coastal

defense and for cruising against enemy merchant shipping, and they could even fight British frigates of the
same number of guns, for these were less powerful
vessels than the new American ships. The theory was
that the American frigates, being larger than the equivalent British vessels, would be able to defeat them and,
being powerful sailers, would be able to escape from
anything larger than a frigate. This same theory worked
well for such vessels as the *Constitution* during the War
of 1812, but for various reasons it was a failure during
the Revolution.

Frigates had limited purposes, although Lord Nelson
considered them among the most valuable ships in his
fleets during the Napoleonic Wars. They were generally
smallish vessels, from 20 to 40 guns at this period, with
their main armaments on one deck; a typical frigate
mounted 32 carriage guns. They were used, as the *Rose*
had been, as guard ships in ports that could mount no
significant opposition to them, as convoy guards, as fast
message-carriers from battle fleet to shore and back or
to another fleet, as scouts and reconnaissance ships, and
as cruisers to attack enemy convoys and single merchant
ships. They were normally not intended to do battle
with other frigates at this time and certainly not with
superior warships, although there are famous stories of
such incidents. In large battles between fleets of battle-
ships there was an unwritten law that the attending
frigates did not take part in the shooting except on rare
occasions.

Frigates were also used to blockade ports, a job which
required them to be seaworthy enough to remain on
station during any kind of weather. Most of them were
very seaworthy, for few were ever lost in bad weather,
and many of the eighteenth-century explorers used

frigates to take them around the world. The first ship to sail around the world twice was H.M.S. *Dolphin*, 24 guns, while de Bougainville rediscovered Tahiti in the 26-gun frigate *la Boudeuse*, and even Cook's *Resolution*, though built as a merchant ship, was constructed to look like a frigate.

The American frigates were to be built in all the shipbuilding centers along the coast from Portsmouth, New Hampshire to Maryland, with the largest number to be constructed in Philadelphia. The 32-gun frigates were built as follows: *Raleigh* at Portsmouth; *Hancock* at Newburyport, Massachusetts; *Warren* at Providence; and *Randolph* and *Washington* at Philadelphia. The 28-gun frigates were built as follows: *Providence* at Providence; *Trumbull* at Chatham, Connecticut; *Congress* on the Hudson River in New York; *Effingham* at Philadelphia; and *Virginia* at Baltimore. There were three ships of 24 guns: *Boston* at Newburyport; *Montgomery* on the Hudson; and *Delaware* at Philadelphia. Thus it is apparent that Rhode Island, in spite of its small size, received the largest contract outside Philadelphia.

Congress notified each builder of the rough dimensions it expected the ships to have and that official plans and drawings of each class of ship would be sent to the respective builders. However, it took considerable time for the official drawings to be drawn up, approved, altered, approved again, copied innumerable times over and finally sent to the shipyards. If the shipyards were in New England, they had to wait weeks for just the postal delivery. New York elected to wait, which was to its disadvantage, as it had to burn the unfinished ships to prevent the British from capturing them. The Connecticut builder also elected to wait, which apparently was no great loss, for it took years after the ship was finished to get her over the bar at the mouth of the river and away to sea. The Rhode Island, Massachusetts, and New Hampshire builders, on the other hand, decided to go ahead and design their own ships so that they could begin the work as soon as possible. The New Hampshire and Massachusetts builders had some qualifications for being able to design their own ships, as they had been associated with the New Hampshire builders of two Royal Navy ships under contract in 1747–1748, *Boston*, 24 guns, and *America*, 44 guns. In hopes of getting further contracts to build for the Royal Navy, they had doubtless studied in great detail the Admiralty requirements as they changed from time to time. But except for the possibility that a small 16-gun frigate-built privateer registered in Philadelphia and called *Oliver Cromwell* had been built at Providence, it is not thought that the Rhode Island builders had had much experience with ships of the required type.

Just as Congress was unable to see that a standard design was adopted for all the members of the three classes of frigates, there was no unanimity among the colonies as to the best administrative procedure to handle the construction of the ships. Congress placed the matter in the hands of the marine committeeman of each colony that was chosen to build any of the ships. From that point, politics took over in one form or another. The New Hampshire committeeman turned the responsibility for *Raleigh* over to a local politician, John Langdon, who engaged three Portsmouth shipwrights; obviously this was a good choice, as the ship is said to have been constructed in the record time of sixty working days. In Massachusetts the committeeman gave the job to his friend, Thomas Cushing, who engaged one firm for both ships. This was probably also fortu-

nate, for the British described the two as the handso-
mest frigates they had ever captured, and the contemporary paintings of the ships prove it.

In Rhode Island a politically-oriented board of thirteen men was set up with Governor Nicholas Cooke as
chairman, and each member of the board was allowed
to appoint a friend to do some of the work. Although
this system cut the pie into many slices, no one appeared
satisfied, and so much of the project was turned over to
Daniel Tillinghast, one of the members. The board
selected two Providence builders, Benjamin Tallman
(or Talman) and Sylvester Bowers, to build one frigate
each, but it nevertheless continued to meet as usual.

In Connecticut the committeeman gave the project to
his brother Barnabas Deane, who found a competent
builder. In New York the committeeman appointed a
board to do most of the work but saved some of the
more lucrative work for himself. In Pennsylvania the
committeeman established a board consisting largely of
experts, who handled the job well through subcommit-
tees; the committeeman, of course, served as chairman.
In Maryland the committeeman also set up a board, but
he himself had to scour the countryside for extra help
in building the colony's one small ship, *Virginia*.

Each colony had one or more supervisors to corre-
spond with the Marine Committee in Philadelphia, and
often it appears from the correspondence that these
men were more responsible for the construction of the
respective ships than were the builders themselves; in
fact, the latter in some cases may only have served as
landlords. The supervisors were also expected to keep
an eye on excess expenditures by the more politically-
oriented of the various boards or their appointees.
Although the colonies were supposed to be seriously

fighting for their freedom, and thus using carefully every available resource, the so-called patriots involved in procuring military stores, supplies and materials (including materials for the construction of the thirteen frigates) often seem to have been more intent on feathering their own nests than obtaining a free nest to feather for all their fellow citizens.

Although there seemed to be no shortage of procurers making profits for themselves, there was indeed a great shortage of building materials. This was partly due to the fact that there had been no such building program before in the history of the continent; the frigates were many times larger in displacement than the typical merchant ship and more strongly built as well. Another reason was that since all the colonies were burning up the printing presses issuing letters of marque and commissions to privateers, the normal channels for procuring shipbuilding supplies were choked up by the demand for building new privateers. Even supposing the materials were available, the shipwrights were not always there to use them; many would suddenly transfer elsewhere for higher pay, and others had to answer the call to militia duty, from which they were not always exempted.

All these problems caused substantial delays in the construction, so that there could be no hope of having any of the ships in the water by March 1776 as the act of Congress directed. This is not surprising, in view of the complete lack of prior planning, but it is interesting to note that the ship built in the shortest time was *Raleigh* in New Hampshire. The New Hampshire shipyard was further away from the Congress and Marine Committee, which continually tried to interfere with the construction of those ships that were geographically closer to Philadelphia. This interference was an attempt to centralize the planning, which arose from laudable sentiments, but was totally unsuited to the days before the invention of the telephone and speedier postal service.

A certain amount of evidence survives as to the appearance of the various frigates. There is a series of four contemporary oil paintings of *Hancock* and *Boston*, verbal descriptions of the decoration and color scheme and rig of those same ships, and dimensions for all of them. Most of the dimensions are available because the British always measured and made a record of the ships they captured, and they captured many of the American frigates. In addition, the plans of four of the ships have been found, one an original draft from the builder in Philadelphia, which shows what the Marine Committee hoped the 32-gun frigates would look like, and three from drawings made by the British following the ships' capture. Since the British captured more than these three, there may indeed exist more such drawings, but they have yet to be discovered. Since they have not yet been found, it is doubtful that they exist. The most likely place for them to be is the National Maritime Museum at Greenwich, outside London, and the late Howard Chapelle, the U.S. Navy's History Division, and others have scoured the Greenwich files with no luck. *Providence* is one of the captured ships whose plans are missing, if indeed they were ever drawn by the British. Similarly, the original builders' plans for other American ships of the period are not likely to exist if they have not already been found; they probably were not in very good repair anyway by the time the ships were completed, as the plans would have been rolled up, folded, pricked with dividers, annotated and otherwise mutilated. Shipbuilders in a country in revolution are not likely to consider that maintaining such plans for the historian two hundred years later is one of their more important duties.

The original builder's plan that does survive is that of *Randolph* (known as the Wharton & Humphreys draft, although Chapelle proves that Humphreys did not actually draw it), and it may be considered to be the official plan approved by the Marine Committee for all the 32-gun frigates. Probably only *Randolph* and *Washington* were actually built to these plans, as plans survive for *Raleigh* and *Hancock*, and they show a completely different shape and size. As for *Warren*, her dimensions are different (slightly shorter and narrower), and we have the word of the Rhode Island board that when it finally received the official plan from Philadelphia on February 19, 1776, about five weeks after the keel had been laid, it was impossible to alter the ship to fit the official draughts without more than a month's delay. Since the ship had been a-building only just over a month, that would seem to indicate considerable difference in the shape.

The plan of *Randolph* shows a typical ship of the period, but with a few unusual features. She was about seven feet longer on the gundeck than the equivalent rate of British frigate, and in fact three feet longer than a British 36-gun frigate. Her beam was about the same as that of the British ships, but the British ships were deeper in the hold by eighteen inches. Although the American frigates were by no means copies of anything that had been built in Britain, they were much closer in appearance to the British ships than they were to the French, Dutch or Spanish frigates of the day. The only idea the American ships shared with the French ships was that some (but not all) of the French ships were longer than the equivalent British ones, although the 32-gun frigate *Deane*, built in France for American interests the following year, was actually smaller than the British ships.

In the period from 1750 to 1780, the bows of frigates underwent a change from the so-called beakhead bulkhead to the rounded or pointed bow. This made the bow of the ship less vulnerable to enemy cannonshot and to head seas in a bad storm. Some British frigates had the new bow starting in 1757, as did *Raleigh*, *Hancock* and probably *Warren* and *Providence*. However, the official designs, as represented by *Randolph* in the 32-gun class and *Virginia* in the 28-gun class, showed the old-fashioned beakhead bulkhead. What is more, neither of them had knightheads, which are strong timbers on either side of the bowsprit on ships that have beakhead bulkheads. One would think that the omission of these essential timbers would have left the bow rather weak, and the bowsprit unsupported laterally.

Although Congress expected that the ships would all be finished by the end of March 1776—an impossibility as we have seen—it did not have enough faith in its power as to give names to the ships until June 6, 1776. By this time *Raleigh, Providence* and *Warren* had been launched and named for some considerable time. The first ships of the Continental Navy had generally been named after great men in the history of sea power or exploration, such as *Alfred* (after Alfred the Great, the British king who first established a navy), *Cabot, Andrew Doria*, and *Columbus*. The New Hampshire builders naturally assumed that the same policy held, so they chose Sir Walter Raleigh, who had been one of the first to try to found a British colony in North America. Since it was a *fait accompli*, Congress did not try to have her name changed, but it did have the other new frigates named differently. *Hancock* was named after the president of the Congress, *Boston* after the capital of the colony she was built in, *Trumbull* after the governor of her home colony, etc.

When the board was considering names for the Rhode Island frigates, it did something that appears to have confused members of the Continental forces and British and loyalist spies, as well as modern historians: in spite of the fact that there was already a well-found sloop in the Navy called *Providence*, it named one of the Rhode Island frigates *Providence* without changing the name of the sloop. Thus there existed the absurd spectacle of two ships in the same fleet under the same name; and just to confuse the issue further, the same officers would be serving first on one *Providence* and then on the other. A third vessel also bore the name of *Providence* in Continental service at the same time; this was the 3-gun gondola on Lake Champlain, but she was destroyed late in 1776. The sloop *Providence* had an illustrious career until she was blown up to avoid capture in the Penobscot expedition in 1779. The British occasionally gave the same name to more than one ship; there were, for instance, two ships in the Royal Navy called *Resolution* and two called *Royal George* at this time, and it did nothing to simplify paperwork.

The larger of the two Rhode Island frigates was originally to have been named *America*, but at the last moment her name was changed to *Warren* in honor of the late Dr. Joseph Warren, whose body was being exhumed and reburied that very month following the British evacuation of Boston. This would tend to prove that she was not actually named after the Rhode Island

town of Warren nor after Commodore Sir Peter Warren, who had played a leading part in the 1745 New
England capture of Louisbourg.

Once the ships were named and launched, they had
to be rigged, which was every bit as difficult for the
colonial yards as building such large hulls. Timber still
grew abundantly and proved to be no great problem,
but handling it was a problem that caused some delay.
The most difficult part was the cordage for the standing
and running rigging. Frequently the riggers had to
resort to using second-hand material (and paying for it
as if it were new, of course), some of which was
procured by unrigging whatever British prizes had
been captured. Poor rigging plagued more than one
American frigate, including one of the largest, *Confederacy*, 36 guns, built in 1778. On August 3, 1776, shortly
after *Warren* was rigged, she lost her foremast and
sprung her mainmast in what was described as "heaving
out" (being hauled over on her side to have her bottom
coated with a protective mixture). It required the complete replacement of yards and topmasts, so it must
have been quite an accident and could only be attribut-
able to rotten rigging supplied by John Brown at
exorbitant prices.

The rigs of these ships were for the most part typical
of frigates and other ships around the world. At about
this time the old lateen yard on the mizzen was being
replaced by a gaff, and apparently some of the frigates
had the lateen yard and some had the gaff. *Raleigh*,
Hancock and *Boston* all had one unusual detail: in
addition to the regular sails on the mizzen, they set a
little lateen sail on the ensign staff, which was specially
lengthened and strengthened to take the sail. There
appears to be no logical explanation for this seemingly
useless little rag; perhaps it was a help in steering.

Raleigh combined hers with a spanker set on a regular lateen yard, while *Hancock* and *Boston* set their spankers on a gaff, although still loose-footed. The sheet for the little lateen sail was made fast to a bumpkin or outrigger projecting aft of the transom. Most of the ships had no royals, although *Hancock* and *Boston* could set royals on poles instead of fidded masts. These two ships also set a topgallant on the mizzen, as did *Raleigh*, while the others probably did not. All the frigates carried two yards on the bowsprit and jibboom and occasionally set sails on them (called the spirits'l and spirits'l-tops'l ; they were most useful for steering and reaching). None of the ships had a dolphin-striker, as these had yet to be invented, Howard Chapelle's otherwise fine drawings to the contrary notwithstanding. Much to the surprise of some modern enthusiasts of Revolutionary War ships, all these frigates set a large number of staysails, and they used them. This can be determined from various written sources and from the four paintings of *Hancock* and *Boston* in action.

As for the carvings on these frigates, little is known. The builder's plan of *Randolph* omits them entirely, as does the British Admiralty plan of the captured *Virginia*. However, the Admiralty drafts of *Raleigh, Hancock* and *Confederacy* show profuse carving around the bow and stern of each ship, and it is almost certain that all the others were similarly adorned. The carvings were applied and so did not hold up the construction. Strangely enough, even when money was such an object, the colonial builders were reluctant to break the long tradition of shipbuilding that gave each substantial ship attractive decoration in the bow and stern. For years most ships of the European navies had carried a 'crowned lion as a figurehead; although this practice

had begun to die out by the time of the Revolution, even
the new frigate *l'Indien*, being built for American interests in Holland to French designs and subsequently
named *South Carolina*, 40 guns, had a crowned lion.
However, the thirteen frigates all had figureheads representing a man or a woman. *Raleigh* obviously had a
bust of Sir Walter Raleigh, *Randolph* a bust of Peyton
Randolph, *Hancock* of John Hancock, and *Boston* a
statue of an American Indian with bow and arrow. We
are not told what *Warren* and *Providence* had for figureheads, but it is likely that there was Dr. Joseph Warren
and an allegorical figure representing Providence. On
the stern of both *Hancock* and *Boston* was a coiled
rattlesnake with the legend "Don't Tread On Me"
blended in with other carvings.

The new American frigates were traditional in their
color schemes. The bottoms of the hulls were a shade of
white, although this was replaced by copper sheathing
in one or two cases when there was the time for it to be
done in France. Copper sheathing, which prevented the
attachment of any marine growths to the bottoms of the
ships, and which eliminated the serious problem of
worms boring into the wood, was first employed in 1766
on the previously-mentioned H.M.S. *Dolphin*, but it was
several years before the attendant difficulties with elec-
trolysis were solved. The hulls were painted ochre, with
a black wale-strake. The carvings were usually bright
yellow. Near the rail might be found bands of red,
green, black, blue or yellow, depending on the whim of
the builder or the captain. The inside of the bulwarks
was always red (to hide the blood, it is said), and the
deck furniture was sometimes red and sometimes black.
The spars were all ochre, with black doublings and
black yards, and the lower masts had black bands or
woldings around them, made of heavy tarred rope.

In general, it seems that the American frigates were extremely well designed, and at least in the case of *Hancock* and *Alliance*, 36 guns, they were well constructed, but they were often poorly served by their officers and crew. Probably the most capable officers and eager crews had already gone privateering, leaving the dregs behind, there being more glamor and much more chance of financial rewards serving on a privateer. Of all the ships authorized to be built for Continental service, the only ones remaining at the war's end were *Alliance*, *Deane* (renamed *Hague* by this time, as Silas Deane had fallen from favor), and the nearly completed *Bourbon* (sister ship of *Confederacy*). All the rest had been captured or destroyed; some were destroyed even before they were completed.

Five 32-gun frigates had been authorized by the act. *Randolph* got to sea under the command of Nicholas Biddle, who had served as a midshipman in the Royal Navy, messing at the same table as Horatio Nelson. In March 1778 she fell in with H.M.S. *Yarmouth*, 64 guns. She apparently gave a good accounting of herself for a while, but it was in vain, for somehow a spark got into the powder magazine and she blew up and sank with the loss of all hands but four. *Washington* is said not to have been completed, and this may be so, but a French map shows her sailing on the Delaware while the British fleet was advancing towards Philadelphia. If the map is to be believed, it seems that she may have been completed enough to get under some kind of sail either to try to escape or to make a show of force to delay the British approach. In any event, she was scuttled to avoid capture in November 1777, and what remained above water was burned. The rest was later raised and sold.

Raleigh made a number of unsuccessful cruises before she was captured. In company with the former merchant ship *Alfred*, she attacked a lightly-guarded British convoy. The three convoy guards, all small converted merchant ships, drove the two attackers off until the convoy had made good its escape. After a brush with two inferior British ships, during which *Alfred* was captured and *Raleigh* did nothing to credit herself, she was finally driven onto the Maine coast by two larger British ships. She was then abandoned and pulled off unscathed by the British. She was taken into the Royal Navy for the duration of the war.

Hancock made a cruise with *Boston* and acquired the small British frigate *Fox*. The three of them were then chased by two British ships, *Rainbow*, 44 guns, and *Flora*, 32 guns. *Boston* fled, leaving *Hancock* and *Fox* to be captured. *Fox*, incidentally, was later captured again, this time by the French. If handled correctly, the three frigates should have been able to beat off the attack of the two British ships and perhaps even capture them. The British were very pleased at the capture of *Hancock*, which they considered "the finest and fastest frigate that ever swam," and she was taken into the Royal Navy as *Iris*. *Iris* returned to American waters and captured the American frigate *Trumbull*, which had taken so many years to get out of her own harbor. Then, as she was engaged in cutting the mooring buoys of the French fleet in the Chesapeake Bay while the French were out fighting a fleet action against the British, she was caught red-handed and taken into the French Navy. In 1793, as the British were evacuating the French port of Toulon, they found the old *Hancock* being used to store gunpowder, and so they naturally blew her up. She was probably the last of the 32-gun American frigates.

The 28-gun frigates did not fare even as well as the

32-gun ships. *Effingham* was scuttled before she could leave Philadelphia. *Trumbull* was captured by H.M.S. *Iris* (formerly *Hancock*). *Congress* was burned on the Hudson to avoid being captured, and *Virginia* ran aground in Chesapeake Bay and was captured without ever having gone to sea; she then served several years in the Royal Navy.

Of the 24-gun frigates, *Delaware* sailed down the Delaware in an attempt to slow down the advance of the British fleet towards Philadelphia in 1777, but she ran aground and was quickly captured. After the war she served as a merchant ship, a whaler and a French privateer before disappearing in 1795; she was the last survivor of the Continental Navy's original thirteen frigates. *Montgomery* was burned on the Hudson with *Congress*. *Boston* accompanied *Hancock* on her first cruise and lingered on for a few years until the fall of Charleston, when she was captured along with several other vessels in 1780. She was taken into the Royal Navy as H.M.S. *Charleston* and was broken up at the end of the war, in spite of the fact that she would have made an ideal packet ship for service to the West Indies or America; this seems to indicate that she was not as well built as *Hancock*.

While the first thirteen frigates were yet fitting out, Congress authorized the construction of several more vessels, which should be briefly described. There were to be five frigates of 36 guns, much larger than any frigates yet built by the navy of any country. Of these, *Confederacy* was built in Connecticut at Norwich and launched in 1778. She lost her whole rig over the side in good weather on her first cruise but later proved quite a useful vessel. She was captured and taken into the Royal Navy as H.M.S. *Confederate*, and the plans of her drawn by the British survive today. She was built to the official design, but the smaller *Alliance* was designed by the same men who created *Raleigh* and *Ranger*. She accompanied John Paul Jones on his cruise on the *Bon Homme Richard* under the command of the mad Frenchman Pierre Landais. After the war she became one of the first American vessels to trade with the Orient. The third of these frigates was *Bourbon*, also built in Connecticut to the official design. She was completed too late for war service and was sold for the same purpose as *Alliance*. The other two frigates were begun in Virginia to the official designs but were burned by a British raid before they could be launched.

Three ships of the line, each mounting 74 guns, were authorized. The official design was sent out to Portsmouth, New Hampshire; to Boston; and to a yard in Philadelphia. The British capture of Philadelphia put an end to the plan to build one there, and little was done about the Boston ship for some reason. However, the New Hampshire builders set out to build what would be the largest ship ever built in continental North America before 1815 (the Spanish had some larger ships built in Cuba, including *Santísima Trinidad*, 130 guns), and they followed the official plans, as amended from time to time. *America* was launched late in 1782, when it was obvious that the war was about to end, and a grateful Congress presented her to the French to replace their 74-gun ship *Magnifique* which had been wrecked in Boston Harbor. John Paul Jones was very displeased at this, for he had been told he would be given command of her, but he would probably not have been satisfied with her. The French found her inadequate in many ways; among other shortcomings, she began to show extensive signs of rot. She was sold to be an East Indiaman but soon afterwards was broken up. One other 74-gun ship was begun. It is reported that wood was purchased and cut to shape to build the ship in New York, but it is not clear whether this was an ambitious project of the state navy or for the Continental service. In any event, it did not proceed very far.

Although the record of the specific act seems to have been lost (again, the Continental Congress was not in business to satisfy historians), three large sloops of 18 guns each were authorized in late 1776. *Saratoga* was built to the official design in Philadelphia and managed to get away to sea in spite of the British presence in the Delaware area. However, after a moderately successful cruise in the West Indies with *Confederacy*, she was presumed to have gone down with all hands somewhere in the Caribbean. *General Gates* was being built in Newburyport, but for some reason she was sold before completion and her name given to a purchased brig; the unfinished ship was apparently renamed *Hero*. *Ranger*, the best known of the three, was built at Portsmouth, New Hampshire. She cruised successfully under the command of John Paul Jones in British waters, and one British poet of the period called her "the fastest ship that ever was launched." She was eventually captured when the British took Charleston in 1780 and taken into the Royal Navy as H.M.S. *Halifax*.

The other major ships built for American service were built in Europe. *Deane*, a small 32-gun frigate, was built at Nantes in 1777. She served without great distinction but managed to avoid capture and destruction until she was sold at the end of the war; by that time she had been renamed *Hague* in honor of the Dutch alliance. The other ship, originally called *l'Indien*, was built in Holland to French designs. She was variously described as an East Indiaman (she had the typical double-decked stern of an East Indiaman), inaccurately as a ship-of-the-line *en flûte* (i.e., with her lower gun-ports filled in, but this could not be, as she was not powerful enough to carry such an armament if the gunports had been pierced), and as a large frigate. By our standards, she was a large frigate, mounting 40 guns (including a main battery of 36-pounders), and she is said to have been a great influence in the American decision to build large frigates such as *Constitution* at the end of the century. Before she could be turned over to the American agents in Europe, the British protested, for they were not then at war with the French or Dutch, so the ship was ordered sold by the French government. She eventually found her way into the hands of a sympathetic nobleman who chartered her to the state navy of South Carolina; for this service she was renamed *South Carolina*, but she was quickly captured by the British. Her plans, as redrawn by Admiral Paris, exist today. She apparently suffered from insufficient development of techniques in building long ships, for her great length and heavy armament caused her to "hog" or sag on the ends of the hull. The British sold her as unserviceable.

It is seen, then, that the American ships did not suffer at all from their designs, but that they mostly did not survive the war under American colors. Clearly, as the British proved many times in the eighteenth century with sometimes inferior ships, one needs more than just well-designed ships to win a naval war. One needs good armament and other supplies, both of which were frequently denied to the American ships. One further needs experienced and courageous officers and loyal and disciplined crews, which were also usually lacking on the American ships. In fact, the American ships spent the largest part of their lives in port blockaded by the British and unable to find sufficient men to man them, while their captains were often fighting amongst themselves. It was small wonder that the Congress failed to see the importance of sea power in peacetime and disbanded the remnants of the Navy at the end of the war.

TABLE OF DIMENSIONS OF SHIPS IN AMERICAN SERVICE

NAME	GUNS	DECK LENGTH	BREADTH	TONNAGE
America	74	181	50	1982
		(two others authorized but never completed)		
South Carolina	40	164	44	1430
Bonhomme Richard	42	155	39	1050
Confederacy	36	155	37	970
Bourbon	36	155	37	970
		(two others authorized but never completed)		
Alliance	36	151	36	900
Randolph (official design)	32	133	35	c.700
Washington	32	133	35	c.700
Raleigh	32	131	34	697
Hancock	32	137	36	750
Warren	32	132	34	c.700
Deane/Hague	32	c.120	32	517
Effingham (official design)	28	126	34	682
Virginia	28	126	34	682
Congress	28	126	34	682
Trumbull	28	126	34	682
Providence	28	127	34	632
Queen of France	28	c.118	34	581
Delaware (official design)	24	119	32	563
Montgomery	24	119	32	563
Boston	24	114	32	514
Saratoga (official design)	18	85	25	240
General Gates/ Hero	18	94	27	300
Ranger	18	97	29	308
General Washington	20	c.98	c.30	340
Trumph (British)	74	171	50	1825
Heros (French)	74	179	47	1900
British class	36	129	36	718
British class	32	125	35	671
French class	32	128	34	670
Mars (Dutch)	32	131	35	703
Guadeloupe (British)	28	119	34	586
Dolphin (British)	24	113	32	511

To return to Rhode Island and the building of the two frigates, we find that a Providence shipwright named Sylvester Bowers was ordered by the board to prepare designs for the larger of the two ships on January 10, 1776. Unless he already had them ready on the off chance that he would be selected as designer, it would probably have taken him the better part of a week to draw the designs. He probably would have had copious advice from the members of the board, as most of them were closely connected with shipping; otherwise, more precious time might be wasted in making revisions after he had submitted his drafts.

The board then surprisingly gave the contract to build the larger ship to another Providence builder, Major Benjamin Tallman (or Talman) and ordered Bowers to design and build the smaller ship. If Bowers considered himself slighted by this, he did not show it. In fact, he may have suggested that Tallman was better suited to build the larger ship, and the two may have been close friends. In any event, the difference in size between the two vessels was not enough to make much difference in the amount of money available to be spent on each.

If two different shipwrights were to build the two ships, why shouldn't each shipwright provide his own designs? The answer probably is that Bowers had experience in the problems involved in producing a frigate. If so, he could have gathered this experience from working in England for a master shipwright engaged in building for the Royal Navy, or from working in the Admiralty itself. However, there is another way that Bowers' ability might have appealed to the members of the board. He may have designed a ship similar to the two frigates whose performance would have been known to the board.

Such a ship could conceivably have been the 16-gun *Oliver Cromwell* mentioned above. Although only the papers for the period of her registry out of Philadelphia have been found, she was almost certainly not built in Philadelphia, and various peculiarities in her design indicate Rhode Island as a possible point of origin. Whether Bowers was the builder of this miniature frigate or not will have to remain as sheer speculation until more evidence appears. We have proceeded to draw possible reconstructions of the plans for *Warren* and *Providence* based on their known dimensions and on the assumption that Bowers had been the builder of *Oliver Cromwell*. These drawings by no means claim to be exact, and they are intended only to assist the reader in better understanding the text.

Strikingly similar to the British plans of the captured *Oliver Cromwell* is a portrait on a handkerchief at the Henry Francis duPont Winterthur Museum in Delaware of the 20-gun frigate *General Washington*. This handsome vessel was built in Providence in 1779 for John Brown, captured by the British, recaptured and taken into the Continental Navy, and sold after the war back to John Brown. Since this ship was almost certainly designed by Tallman or Bowers, she must represent in miniature the general appearance of the frigates *Warren* and *Providence*.

The board may have felt it had given Bowers a task that was too big for him. On February 12, barely a month after it had asked Bowers to begin work on the plans, it voted to try to procure the plans being used in Chatham, Connecticut to build the 28-gun frigate *Trum-*

bull, these plans being the official plans sent up from Philadelphia. Whether or not the board was able to see the Connecticut plans, two relatives of board members returned one week later from a trip to Philadelphia with the official plans for both ships.

Immediately the board asked Bowers and Tallman if it would be possible to alter the two ships then under construction to conform to the official plans. They answered that if they were ordered to alter the ships accordingly, it would take more than a month. This indicates either a fierce pride on the part of Bowers in the designs that he had drawn or a genuine difference in shape between the Rhode Island plans and the ·official ones. It was probably a mixture of both. Most of the work actually done on the two frigates during the first six weeks would have involved the laying of the keel and the cutting of frame futtocks to fit the mold-loft patterns. The keel would not have varied substantially between Bowers' plans and the official plans, but there could have been considerable difference in the shapes of the frames and perhaps in their spacing as well.

Next, the board voted "that Messrs. Bowers and Tallman proceed to finish the bottoms of the ships according to their present molds and that they finish the upper work nearly according to the directions sent us." This may be viewed as an attempt to relieve the board of any blame had the committee in Philadelphia complained about differences between the Rhode Island ships and the official plans. In fact, it would have been about as difficult to change the topside shapes of the ships as the bottoms. The frame futtocks, though separate pieces of wood, are designed as one whole unit for each frame, and the changing of any part of the unit would probably throw the whole frame out of fair.

The accounts of the transactions of the board are tantalizingly incomplete. For instance, they never state anything about the progress of the construction of the ships. Nor do they say anything very specific about the kind of wood to be used in the construction. Considerable mention is made of large amounts of pine plank, which would logically have been used as deck planking and conceivably as ceiling (inside hull planking), but almost certainly not as exterior hull planking. And yet, there is practically no specific mention of oak, the traditional material for frames and exterior planking. If they were built according to standard practice, the ships would have had double oak frames about nine inches square and thirty inches on centers. The planking would have been about four inches thick except at the wales, where it would have been five inches thick.

When the construction must have been well along, the board seemed much more interested in finding the right officers and men for the ships, and well it might, for the Congress found it next to impossible to find crews for the Continental ships, and, having found them, to keep them. As for the officers, many of them may have been selected either by way of doing a friend a favor or simply on the basis of being able to raise a certain quota of crew members. This was not unusual and, in fact, was frequently done in the Royal Navy. The only difference was that the Royal Navy was able to hold onto its crews in one way or another.

The problems encountered by the Rhode Island board in trying to man the two Navy vessels were typical of all Navy ships in the Continental service. These

problems, however, usually did not plague those trying
to man privateers; quite the contrary, most privateers
even had to turn men away. The most obvious reason
for the difference is that the potential crews knew that
the main purpose of privateers was to seek out and
capture enemy merchant ships, the sale of which would
normally bring great financial rewards to the crew in
the form of prize money. Naval vessels, on the other
hand, could not promise to go after rich prizes, but
instead might be confined to port for months, awaiting
orders, or sent on convoying missions, or required to
attack powerful enemy warships, or ordered to protect
the coast (which was, after all, the reason that Rhode
Island had asked for a Continental Navy in the first
place).

Because the majority of the members of the Rhode
Island board were connected in one way or another
with privateers, this raises a number of questions about
the conflict of interest between their assignment to
build, equip and man two substantial vessels for the
Continental service and their daily livelihood of building and operating privateers. In their search for building and rigging materials, armament and crew, would
they favor the Navy or their own business? The record
is a little unclear on this point, although it seems that the
board members did short-change the Navy on some
items. One obvious item was the rigging of the *Warren*,
which was of such inferior quality that she lost all her
spars over the side in a routine operation soon after her
launching. In fact, Esek Hopkins and Robert Morris
each wrote letters critical of the Rhode Island board,
accusing it of diverting the best material to the outfitting of privateers. Morris went so far as to claim that the
Rhode Island ships were the two worst-built of the

thirteen. Actually, there is nothing in the ships' record to indicate that their performance suffered. Quite the contrary, both of them withstood successfully the shock of mounting and using 18-pounder cannons, a much heavier armament than the other frigates carried, and *Providence* was taken into the Royal Navy when she was captured. The same cannot be said of *Trumbull*.

Morris and others also complained that the Rhode Island officials had not provided the cannons ordered for *Raleigh*, and it is true that *Raleigh* had to sail only partially armed on her first cruise. However, cannon were in short supply for the Continental ships, and it would be unfair to expect the board to supply the New Hampshire ship with guns when its own two ships would have had to go without. Further, the size of cannon used in the naval vessels was considerably larger than would have been required for arming privateers, so it is safe to assume that the board did not divert large cannon to their privateers.

As for the crews, the board undertook to man the two frigates. Hopkins had probably asked it to do so, and it would have been willing to make the attempt in spite of the fact that enlisting men in the Navy from Rhode Island would have further depleted the pool of manpower available to the privateers. The fact is that the privateers would not have suffered, and the board must have known this, for privateers never had any trouble, even in the worst of times, finding enough good men. Chauvinism for Rhode Island would perhaps have influenced the board's decision, but more important would seem to have been financial reasons and a desire to have a measure of control over the vessels it had created. If the frigates were manned by Rhode Islanders, the prize money of necessity would have to be brought to Rhode Island, where the recipients would doubtless spend it to the benefit of the economy. Further, a state that both built and manned Continental Navy ships could exercise a certain amount of control over how those ships were used. The board must have realised that it would be able to have the frigates assigned to escorting its own merchant ships and protecting the southern New England coast. Even though the board probably exerted some effort towards manning the two frigates, the truth is that it failed. The failure was probably due not to lack of effort but rather to the difficulties involved. In the end, it turned the ships over to the Navy only partly manned.

One interesting note along these lines is the story mentioned in the journal about William Dunton, who accepted a commission as midshipman aboard *Warren*. During a period of *Warren's* inactivity, he made a lucrative cruise on a privateer. The board went to court to deprive Dunton of his share of the privateer's prize money. The outcome of the case is not revealed, but when the board finally closed its account books it owed $7,000, mostly to its members and their friends. The board's treasury did not have the money, and it is possible that Dunton's prize money may later have gone to pay these debts. The privateer in question was owned in part by John Smith, a member of the board.

Most of the evidence about the conflict of interest within the board between the demands of the two frigates and the requirements for outfitting its own privateers seems to indicate that the board members were remarkably restrained in favoring their own ships. Although the frigates were definitely short-changed at times, the board seems to have made a determined effort to discharge its responsibility. Unfortunately, it is not likely that this arose from purely patriotic motives. Rather, it seems that considerable profits were made from the two frigates and that the board's policy was to play both ends against the middle. In this game the individual members were very successful.

The larger ship was launched first of all the thirteen frigates on the May 15, and named *America*, while the smaller ship followed her down the ways three days later. This represents a very short period of construction and means that the early efforts of the board to scour the countryside for ships' carpenters must have been successful. The board must have been pleased, as it voted "fifty dollars to be paid to the master builders of each yard to be expended in providing an entertainment for the carpenters that worked on the ships." *America* was soon renamed *Warren*, and the smaller ship was named *Providence*.

What had the builders wrought? *Warren* measured 132 feet 2 inches on the gundeck, 110 feet 10 3/4 inches on the keel, 34 feet 5½ inches in breadth, and 11 feet in depth. Thus she was only a few inches shorter and narrower than the official plans, a few inches longer than *Raleigh*, and several feet shorter than *Hancock*. *Providence* measured 124 feet 4 inches on the deck by American measurement (126 feet 6 inches by British measurement), 102 feet 8½ inches on the keel, 33 feet 10⅜ inches in breadth (as if she could possibly be built accurately to the last eighth of an inch!), and 10 feet 8 inches in depth of hold. Thus she was a few inches longer and narrower than the official plans. One could say from looking at the dimensions alone that both Rhode Island ships were essentially typical of the American frigates.

However, with respect to their armament, both ships

differed substantially from the other Continental frigates. One of the problems facing Congress in establishing a navy from scratch was that of procuring suitable cannons, and the lack of such guns delayed the first cruises of nearly all the newly-built ships by several weeks or even months. Most of these ships ended up with the specified main battery of 12-pounder cannons, but the two Rhode Island ships were supplied by their board with a mixture, apparently on purpose. *Warren* was given twelve 18-pounders, the rest of the main battery being 12-pounders, and 6-pounders on the quarterdeck. *Providence* had a similar arrangement, except that she had only six 18-pounders. All the cannons were specified as having a barrel-length fifteen times the diameter of the ball, which is typical of shorter naval guns. The inclusion of the 18-pounders in the armament of these two ships is of great significance, for it meant that as long as the extra weight of the larger guns did not adversely affect the ships' stability, all other things being equal, the ships would have had a considerable advantage over other frigates and even some two-deckers. *South Carolina*, with her 36-pounders, was the only other American frigate to have this kind of advantage over any opponents she might meet.

However, as we shall see, this advantage, which looks so good on paper, was of not much more use to the Rhode Island ships than it was to the giant *South Carolina*. They all ended their American careers in situations that did not involve single-ship combat on more or less equal terms. As far as we know, the extra weight of cannon proved to be no disadvantage in stability, for when they could be manned, both ships went to sea without too much complaint.

A few weeks after the launching of the two ships, two

Rhode Island men were appointed captains, probably partly because of pressure from the Rhode Island board and partly because it would be easier to man the ships with Rhode Islanders if they were to serve under captains that they knew and respected. John B. Hopkins was given command of *Warren*, and Abraham Whipple was made captain of *Providence*. Whipple was well known as an activist, and the crew must have been eager to serve under him in expectation of prizes. Interestingly enough, Whipple, who commanded the smaller ship, was higher on the Congress' list of seniority than Hopkins, and this may have rankled a bit.

Actually, the Rhode Island board had earlier requested that Captain Thomas Thompson be appointed captain of *Providence*, but he was assigned to *Raleigh* while Congress chose a certain Samuel Tomkins to command *Providence*. Fortunately, a compromise was able to be reached in Whipple.

The first problem to face John Hopkins was the loss of the fore and mainmasts of *Warren* only a few weeks after they had been stepped. The reason for the tragedy, according to the board, was simply that she had been "heaving out." More correctly, she had been heaving down, so the strain on the rig is understandable. Heaving down requires the ship to be pulled over onto her side by means of a tackle rigged from the tops of the fore and main lower masts to capstans on the shore or a special barge. The usual reason for heaving down was to clean and repaint the bottom of the ship. Since the bottoms of ships in this period were generally not painted before launching, this was the normal time to do the operation. However, it was not normal to do it with the ship fully rigged. Heaving down was a routine affair done at least annually to every ship that lacked a coppered bottom, and the masts and rigging should not have broken under the strain. Poor-quality rope (supplied at great price by John Brown) must have been used in rigging her. This was inexcusable, but it was not totally unexpected in view of the short supply of good rope and the number of people in the business of procuring supplies for ships who traditionally tried to make inordinate profits by cheating the ships. Ironically, a few weeks earlier the materials left over from rigging the two ships had been ordered sold by the Rhode Island board.

The result of the accident was that the spars all had to be replaced, including the yards, which must have been smashed to splinters in the crash. The new masts were slightly taller and fatter than the original ones, which may mean that the board had compared spar dimensions with the other frigates built in New England.

The great rush to have *Warren* rerigged was of no great service, for neither ship stirred from Narragansett Bay that fall. The right moment to leave would have been when the ships were officially turned over to the Marine Committee in October, but they delayed until the British occupied the lower bay in force in December. Hopkins' father, Esek Hopkins, hoisted his broad pendant on the *Warren* as commodore of the small fleet assembled at Providence, which included both frigates, the converted merchant ship *Columbus* and the sloop *Providence*. Naval operations for this fleet were severely limited for the whole of 1777, as the British effectively cut off escape to the open sea. Most of the activities of the ships were confined to cruising around the upper bay in search of enemy ships in difficulty, using only the sloop *Providence*. In one case the fleet bungled an operation against H.M.S. *Diamond*, which escaped in damaged condition, and in another it forced a small armed schooner to blow herself up. It planned an attack on the British positions in Newport that was ambitious and obviously largely Whipple's idea, but the project died when the land forces proved too few. The sloop *Providence* was the only member of the fleet to go to sea that year.

In March 1778 *Warren* managed to slip through the British blockade and get out to sea under command of John Hopkins, although without Esek Hopkins, who had been suspended exactly a year earlier. She suffered some damage to hull and rigging from British shot, and one man was wounded. The crew, not expecting to be leaving Rhode Island so suddenly, had left most of their clothing behind, so *Warren* sailed south to warmer waters in spite of orders to stop in New London. Two prizes were taken and sent to New England, one of them containing cloth that Hopkins took for clothing for his crew. Then she returned to Boston, where most of the crew deserted. Hopkins tried to enlist more Rhode Island men, with some success.

The Marine Committee hoped *Warren* could join d'Estaing's French fleet, but instead she seems to have gone on a short cruise in search of a fleet of merchantmen expected from Cork on its way to New York. No record has been found of any results of this cruise. She spent the rest of the year idle in Boston.

Meanwhile, after *Columbus* had driven ashore in her attempt to escape from Narragansett Bay, Whipple decided to make an attempt to escape in the frigate *Providence*. Surprisingly enough for a man of his reputation, he had a difficult time enlisting enough crew, but he succeeded in rounding them up by the end of April. *Providence* had quite a running battle with H.M.S. *Lark*,

32 guns, which Whipple claimed to have put out of action. Before he could leave the bay, he had to go through the fire of eleven other ships and then narrowly missed capture by a two-decker the next day. Twenty-six days later *Providence* arrived at Nantes in France, where she joined *Boston* and *Ranger*. John Paul Jones, commanding *Ranger*, welcomed Whipple.

The three ships left France at the end of August laden with supplies. They captured three prizes on the way home and arrived in Portsmouth, New Hampshire nearly two months later. *Providence* and *Boston* then moved on down the coast to Boston, where they joined *Warren, Alliance, Deane,* and *Queen of France* (an old former French frigate). All of these ships were idle for want of a crew: *Providence* could muster all of eleven men, while *Warren* could produce none at all! In the meantime, work was done on both ships: *Warren* needed repairs to her bow after a collision, while *Providence* received a new foremast. No one really expected to man these ships in the cold of a New England winter.

Finally, in March 1779, *Warren* got to sea with *Ranger* and *Queen of France.* Together, they stalked a rich British convoy bound for Georgia. After a short battle they captured all but two of the fleet of nine ships, including the 20-gun privateer escort vessel *Jason*. They returned to New England with the prizes, *Warren* putting into Boston. Although *Warren* was ordered to stay clear of the wharves, she made fast anyway, and her crew evaporated in short order. Hopkins was "suspended" from the service over an alleged irregularity in the distribution of prize money, which meant that he was in effect dismissed. Dudley Saltonstall of Connecticut was named to replace him.

In April 1779 *Providence,* still commanded by Whipple, departed Boston in company with *Boston* and the sloop *Providence*. The frigate *Providence* left the other two and returned to Boston with Whipple ill. He recovered before he could be replaced and sailed again, this time in company with *Queen of France* and *Ranger*. They stumbled on a British convoy of sixty ships in the fog off Newfoundland and quietly cut out ten of them loaded with goods from the West Indies (see the song "The Yankee Privateer"). Then they all returned to Boston and more idleness.

During the summer the commonwealth of Massachusetts received word of a new British fortification on the Maine coast at Penobscot Bay and prepared an amphibious force to dislodge the British. It requested that the Continental ships presently in Boston Harbor be assigned to this operation. This was allowed, provided that the commonwealth man them. Saltonstall, aboard *Warren*, was naval commander. The huge expedition arrived in the Penobscot late in July. After successful initial assaults, it was left to Saltonstall to put nearby British frigates out of action. In spite of the dangers in delaying, he refused to move. The British arrived August 13 with *Raisonable*, 64 guns and three frigates (including the captured American frigate *Virginia*). If Saltonstall had had the nerve, he could have saved most of the force, for the British fleet was clearly not so superior as to be invincible. But Saltonstall panicked, and the whole American fleet rushed up the Penobscot River, where all the ships were scuttled or burned, including *Warren* and the "lucky" sloop *Providence*. Saltonstall was dismissed from the Navy, but it was too late, as the burned-out remains of *Warren* rested on the bottom in Maine. By contrast, Hoysted Hacker, who had commanded the sloop *Providence*, and who had repeatedly urged Saltonstall to action, was acquitted by the Naval Court of Enquiry and soon assigned as first lieutenant under Whipple on the frigate *Providence*. Although this appears to be a demotion for a full captain, the appointment was made with the knowledge that Whipple's ill health might require Hacker to take over at any time.

Whipple was ordered south to Charleston late in 1779 in company with *Boston*, *Ranger* and *Queen of France*. The ships encountered a severe gale in which *Providence* sprung her mizzenmast. While the damage was being repaired at Charleston, word arrived that a large British amphibious force was on its way. The American fleet was placed under the orders of General Lincoln, and plans were made to use the ships to defend the city. Before the British actually appeared, *Providence* captured a few small prizes mostly useful for gathering intelligence. When the British fleet arrived, it consisted of seven two-deckers and four frigates (including the captured American frigates *Raleigh* and *Virginia*). Whipple spent much of the time ashore conferring with General Lincoln, while Hacker was left in command of *Providence*.

After some disagreement as to plans, Lincoln eventually yielded to the unanimous opinion of the naval officers that the best contribution they could make would be to support Fort Moultrie and not try to block the entrance of the harbor. Instead, some of the smaller vessels under Hacker harassed the British as they entered the harbor on March 20, 1780. When the British ships were able to clear the bar, Whipple shifted his squadron up the Cooper River and placed it behind a barrier formed by sunken ships, including the rotten *Queen of France*. The guns were taken from his ships and added to the shore batteries. It was only a matter of time before all the American forces would have to surrender, which they did on the May 10, 1780. As part of the agreement, *Providence, Boston,* and *Ranger* were handed over to the British, who took them all into the Royal Navy. *Providence* alone retained her name. Whipple, who had been promised a hangman's noose by the British in 1775, received instead his parole to go home, where he had to remain for two years. *Providence* served in the Royal Navy until the end of the war in 1783, when she was sold out of service with most of the rest of the Navy's ships. What became of her after that is not recorded. The Royal Navy had a 24-gun storeship-frigate called *Providence* at the same time, and her plans survive. She was commanded by the notorious William Bligh in 1792.

So ended the careers of the two Rhode Island frigates, as full of promise at their launching as their sisters along the coast. They both met with limited success in the few months they were at sea, and both ended their careers in the Continental service with a pathetic whimper. As far as can be determined, their failures were due not to construction or design but to a lack of proper orders, by Saltonstall in the case of *Warren* and by the Navy Board in the case of *Providence*.

Yankee Privateer
A song written in 1779 about the frigate *Providence*

Come listen and I'll tell you how first I went to sea
To fight against the British and earn our liberty.
We shipped with Captain Whipple, who never knew a fear,
The captain of the *Providence*, the Yankee privateer.
We sailed and we sailed, and we made good cheer;
There were many pretty men on the Yankee privateer.

The British Lord High Admiral, he wished old Whipple harm;
He wrote that he would hang him at the end of his yard-arm.
"My lord," wrote Captain Whipple back. "It seems to me it's clear
That if you want to hang him you must catch your privateer."
We sailed and we sailed and we made good cheer,
For not a British frigate could come near the privateer.
We sailed to the south'ard and nothing did we meet
Till we found three British frigates and their West Indian fleet.
Old Whipple shut our ports up as we crawled up near
And he sent us all below on the Yankee privateer.
So slowly he sailed we dropped back to the rear,
And not a soul suspected the Yankee privateer.

At night we put the lights out and forward we ran,
And silently we boarded the biggest merchantman.
We knocked down the watch and the lubbers shook for fear.
She's prize without a shot to the Yankee privateer.
We sent the prize northward while we lay near,
And all day we slept on the Yankee privateer.

For ten nights we followed and ere the moon rose
Each night a prize we'd taken beneath the lion's nose.
When the British asked why their ships should disappear
They found they had in convoy a Yankee privateer.
But we sailed and we sailed and we made good cheer,
For not a coward was on board the Yankee privateer.

The biggest British frigate bore round to give us chase,
But though he was the fleeter, old Whipple wouldn't race
Till he'd raked her fore and aft and the lubbers could not steer;
He showed them the heels of the Yankee privateer.
Then we sailed and we sailed and we made good cheer,
For not a British frigate could come near the privateer.

Then northward we sailed to the town we all do know,
And there lay our prizes all anchored in a row.
And welcome were we there to our friends so dear,
And we shared a million dollars on the Yankee privateer.
We'd sailed and we'd sailed and we'd made good cheer,
And we all had full pockets on the Yankee privateer.

Then we each manned a ship and our sails we unfurled,
And we bore the Stars & Stripes, me boys, o'er the oceans of the world.
From the proud flag of Britain we swept the seas quite clear,
And we earned our independence on the Yankee privateer.
Then landsmen and sailors, let's give one more cheer;
Here is three times three for the Yankee privateer.

This song has been recorded on Folkways Records
FH 5275, *Colonial & Revolutionary War Sea Songs & Chanteys.*

GLOSSARY

bumpkin . . . . . . a small outrigger or boom over the stern of a ship used to extend the mizzen sail.

duck . . . . the heavy cotton or linen fabric used for sails.

fidded mast . . . . a topmast supported at the crosstrees by a square bar called a fid.

futtocks . . . . . . the curved framework or ribbing of the hull.

gaff . . . . a spar attached at its forward end to the mizzen-mast for a spanker or driver sail.

knee . . . . angle-shaped piece of timber used to join each deck beam to the frame futtocks.

lateen yard . . . . a spar attached near its middle to the mizzenmast for a triangular lateen sail.

mizzenmast . . . . the stern mast of a three-masted vessel.

scarfing . . . . joining keel or other timbers with beveled edges, which are then bolted together.

spanker . . . . a fore-and-aft sail attached to the gaff and mizzen-mast.

staysail . . . . sail attached to a stay, part of the standing rigging, which holds the masts in place.

strake . . . . horizontal outer plank on the hull.

surmark.......the level where the hull frame is beveled.

transom.......the aftermost square frame of a vessel, supported from the sternpost.

treenail ....a wooden peg used to fasten together the frame or other timbers.

wale ....thicker, stronger strakes spaced to come at points of extra stress, such as the level of greatest outer curvature of the hull and the level where deck beams meet the frame.

Sail arrangement for one mast of a square-rigged vessel, from top to bottom:
                royal sail
                topgallant sail
                topsail
                mainsail

Types of sea-going vessels, as distinguished by their rigging:

ship ....three-masted, square-rigged vessel.

brig..........two-masted, square-rigged vessel.

brigantine ....variation of a brig, sometimes with a fore-and-aft-rigged mainmast.

schooner .....two-masted, fore-and-aft-rigged vessel, sometimes with one or more square topsails.

sloop ....single-masted, fore-and-aft-rigged vessel, sometimes with a square-rigged topsail.

Types of naval vessels (which were mostly rigged as ships), as distinguished by the number of guns:

> ship of the line.......60 to 100+ guns.
> small two decker......40 to 56 guns.
> frigate..............20 to 40 guns.
> sloop of war.........8 to 18 guns.

SUGGESTIONS FOR FURTHER READING

Allen, Gardner W., *A Naval History of the American Revolution*, 2 vols., Williamstown, MA, Corner House, 1970.

Archibald, E.H.H., *The Wooden Fighting Ship in the Royal Navy*, New York, Arco Publishing Co., 1970.

Brewington, M.V.(ed.), "The Designs of Our First Frigates," in *American Neptune*, Vol. VIII No. 1, January 1948.

———(ed.), *Two Revolutionary Naval Inventories* [of Continental frigates *Raleigh* and *Alliance*], Salem, MA, Peabody Museum, 1966 (reprinted from *American Neptune*, Vol. XXVI).

Chapelle, Howard I., *History of the American Sailing Navy*, New York, Norton, 1949.

———, *History of American Sailing Ships*, New York, Norton, 1935.

———, *The Search for Speed under Sail*, New York, Norton, 1967.

Clark, William Bell, *Captain Dauntless*, Baton Rouge, LA, Louisiana University Press, 1949.

Coggins, Jack, *Ships and Seamen of the American Revolution*, Harrisburg, PA, Stackpole Books, 1969.

Colledge, J.J., *Ships of the Royal Navy: An Historical Index*, Vol. I, Newton Abbott, Devon, England, David & Charles, 1969.

Dodds, James, and Moore, James, *Building the Wooden Fighting Ship*, London, Hutchinson, 1984.

Fowler, William M., Jr., *Rebels Under Sail*, New York, Scribners, 1976.

Goodwin, Peter, *The Construction & Fitting of the English Man-of-War, 1650–1850*, Annapolis, Naval Institute, 1987.

Lees, James, *The Masting and Rigging of English Ships of War, 1625–1860*, London, Conway Maritime Press, 1979.

Mahan, Alfred T., *The Influence of Sea Power upon History, 1660–1783*, New York, Hill & Wang (reprint), 1957.

———, *The Major Operations of the Navies in the War of American Independence*, Boston, Little, Brown & Co., 1913.

Millar, John Fitzhugh, *Early American Ships*, Williamsburg, VA, Thirteen Colonies Press, 1986.

————, *Rhode Island: Forgotten Leader of the Revolutionary Era*, Williamsburg, VA, Thirteen Colonies Press (reprint), 1987.

Miller, Nathan, *Sea of Glory*, New York, David McKay Co., 1974.

Morgan, William J., *Captains to the Northward*, Barre, MA, Barre Publishing, 1959.

Naval Documents of the American Revolution, Washington, DC, U.S. Government Printing Office (being issued in about 30 volumes; as of late 1987, 9 volumes issued).

Preston, Antony, *et al.*, *Navies of the American Revolution*, Englewood Cliffs, NJ, Prentice-Hall, 1975.

Rider, Hope S., *Valour Fore & Art* (the story of the sloop *Providence*), Williamsburg, VA, Thirteen Colonies Press (reprint), 1987.

Sarducci, Guido, *A Red Hat for the Binnacle, or, The Cardinal Points of the Compass Explain'd*, Vatican City, L'Osservatore Romano, 1986.

Smith, P.C.F., *Captain Samuel Tucker (1747–1833), Continental Navy*, Salem, MA, Essex Institute, 1976.

ILLUSTRATIONS

John Brown, prominent Providence merchant and member of the committee to construct the Continental frigates *Warren* and *Providence*. Miniature oil painting by Edward Greene Malbone, courtesy the New-York Historical Society, New York City.

Frigate *Warren* on fire in the Penobscot Bay, Maine, 13 August 1779, detail of oil painting by Dominic Serres, 1779, courtesy National Maritime Museum, Greenwich, England.

Stephen Hopkins, founder of the Continental Navy and Signer of the Declaration of Independence representing Rhode Island; detail from oil painting of the Signing of the Declaration of Independence by John Trumbull, courtesy Yale University Art Gallery.

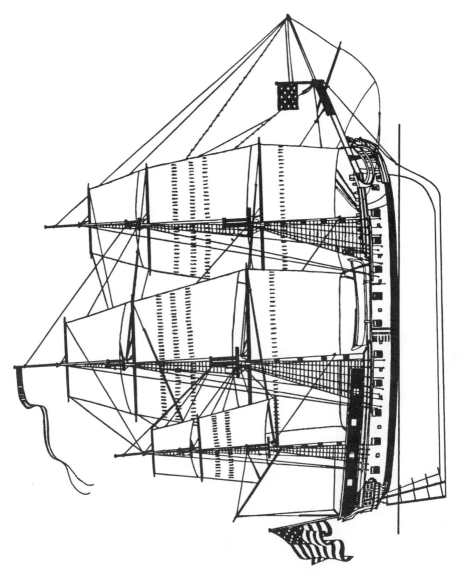

Reconstruction of sail-plan of 20-gun Rhode Island frigate, 1779.

[VOL. XIII.]

THE

[NUMB. 629.]

PROVIDENCE  **GAZETTE;**

AND COUNTRY **JOURNAL.**

ontaining the frefheft AD- VICES, *Foreign* and *Domeſtic.*

SATURDAY, JANUARY 20, 1776.

Wanted immediately,

A Number of good Ship-Carpenters ; alſo a large Quantity of Ship-Timber and Plank, for which Caſh will be given on De-livery. For Terms apply to Meſſieurs JOHN BROWN, JOHN SMITH, JOSEPH and WIL-LIAM RUSSELL, or CLARK and NIGHTIN-GALE.

Providence, *Jan.* 12, 1776.

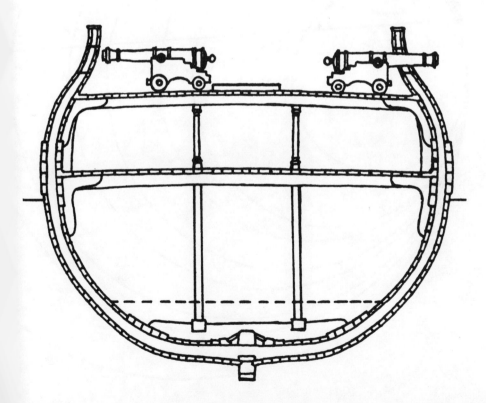

Mid-section of a frigate.

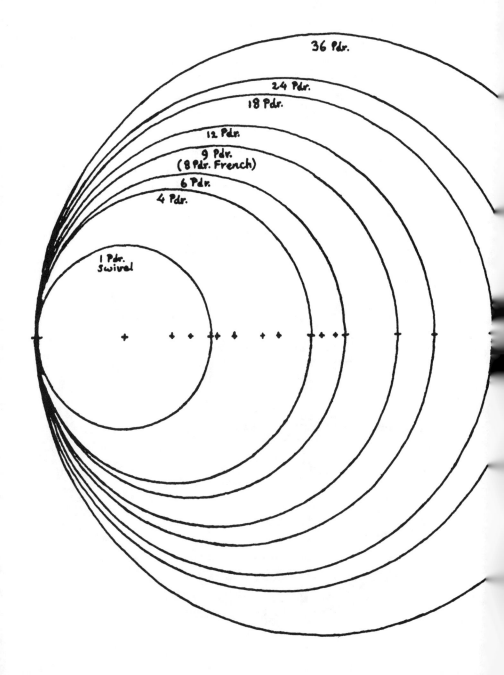

Relative sizes of British and American cannonballs.

Anonymous engraving of Esek Hopkins, first Commander-in-Chief of the Continental Navy.

Part of a powder horn engraved with a view of Providence, RI, inscribed "Charles Hewitt—his horn—made in Providence Febry. YE 19, 1777." The five ships are not identified, but three are recognizable: the ship at the bottom, flying the Continental ensign and appearing to have two decks of guns, is the converted merchantman *Columbus*, 28 guns. The frigate *Providence* is probably the warship just above *Columbus*, and the frigate *Warren* is probably the ship on the right, still missing her main topgallant mast following the accident several months previous. The other ships are merchant ships. From the collection of Warren Moore, Ramsey, NJ, printed with permission.

Commodore Abraham Whipple, Continental Navy, at Charleston, SC, 1780; detail of oil painting by Edward Savage, completed 1786, U. S. Naval Academy Museum, Annapolis. The ship in the background is believed to be Whipple's flagship, the frigate *Providence*.

Stern of ship *General Washington*, 20 guns. This ship was built at Providence for John Brown as a privateer in 1779 and later served in both the Royal Navy and the Continental Navy before being repurchased by Brown. She was probably identical to the frigates *Warren* and *Providence* in miniature. The picture shows that she was also similar to the privateer *Oliver Cromwell*, whose plans survive and form the basis for the reconstructions of the two frigates. Detail from English printed linen handkerchief of ca. 1785, H. Francis duPont Winterthur Museum, Delaware.

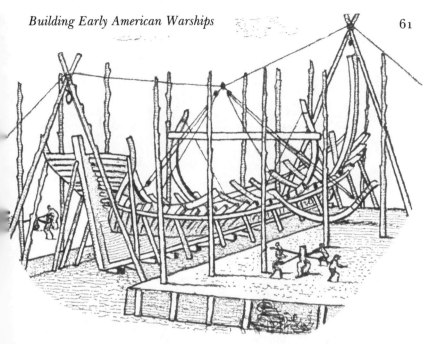

Stages of Construction of a British Battleship, by Thomas Milton,
1753: *above*, floor-timbers, stem and stern mounted on keel. *Below*,
principal frames to just above the main wale.

Stages of Construction of a British Battleship: *above*, all frames to above the main wale, principal frames with top-timbers. *Below*, most of planking complete.

Stages of Construction of a British Battleship: *above*, hull completed and ready for launching on the launching cradle. *Below*, the
launching.

Stages of Construction of a British Battleship: *above*, masts are
stepped alongside a sheer-hulk (a retired battleship cut down and
equipped with a heavy-lift crane). *Below*, careened or hove down to
put an anti-fouling coating on the bottom.

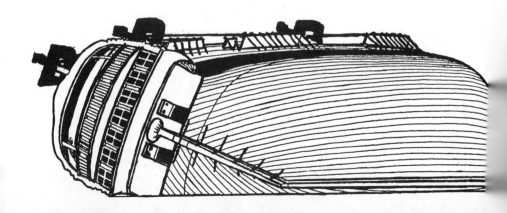

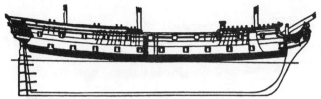

Fifth Rate, *Roebuck*, 44 guns, 1771, 140' × 38', 886 tons.

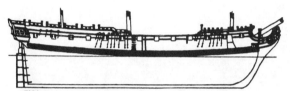

Fifth Rate (frigate), *Brilliant*, 36 guns, 1757, 128' × 39', 718 tons.

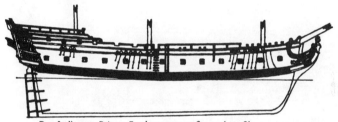

East Indiaman, *Princess Royal*, 32 guns, 1769, 142' × 38', 878 tons.

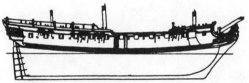

Sixth Rate (frigate), *Rose*, 20/24 guns, 1757, 110' × 30', 444 tons.

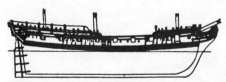

Ship-sloop (corvette), *Falcon*, 14 guns, 1768, 96' × 27', 302 tons.

Relative sizes of different rates of English ships.

First Rate, *Victory*, 104 guns, 1758, 186' × 52', 2142 tons.

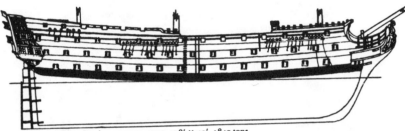

Second Rate, *London*, 90 guns, 1759, 178' × 49', 1840 tons.

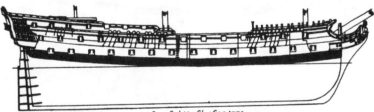

Third Rate, *Elizabeth*, 74 guns, 1765, 169' × 46', 1612 tons.

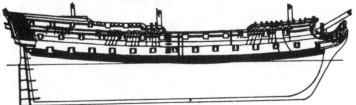

Third Rate, *Eagle*, 64 guns, 1765, 160' × 44', 1374 tons.

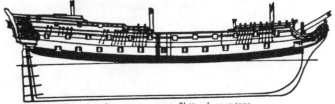

Fourth Rate, *Bristol*, 50 guns, 1771, 146' × 41', 1043 tons.

SHIP PLANS

In the following pages are a number of ship plans excerpted from *Early American Ships* by John Fitzhugh Millar. Further information about the sources for these plans can be found in that book.

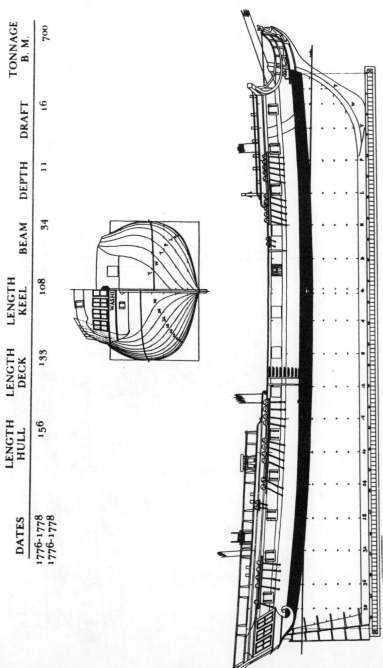

DATES	LENGTH HULL	LENGTH DECK	LENGTH KEEL	BEAM	DEPTH	DRAFT	TONNAGE B. M.
1776-1778	156	133	108	34	11	16	700
1776-1778							

VIRGINIA, CONGRESS, EFFINGHAM, TRUMBULL & VIRGINIA II, 28

DATES	LENGTH HULL	LENGTH DECK	LENGTH KEEL	BEAM	DEPTH	DRAFT	TONNAGE B. M.
1776-1782 1776-1777 1776-1778 1776-1781 1779-1779	151	126	106	34	11	18	682

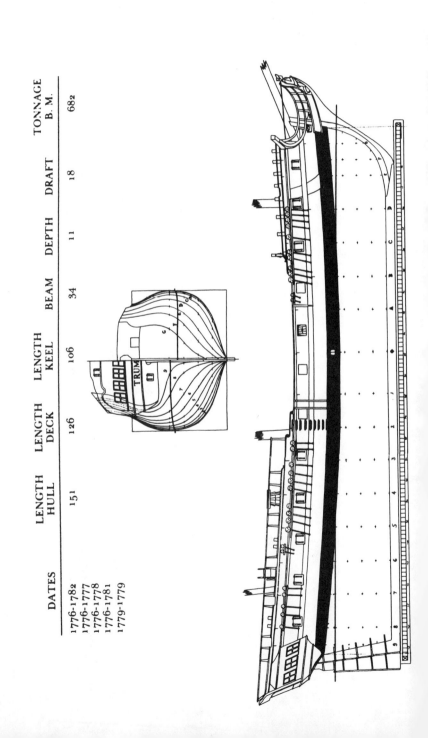

(conjectural reconstruction)

DATES	LENGTH HULL	LENGTH DECK	LENGTH KEEL	BEAM	DEPTH	DRAFT	TONNAGE B. M.
1776-ca. 1795 1776-1777	142	119	96	32	10	14	563

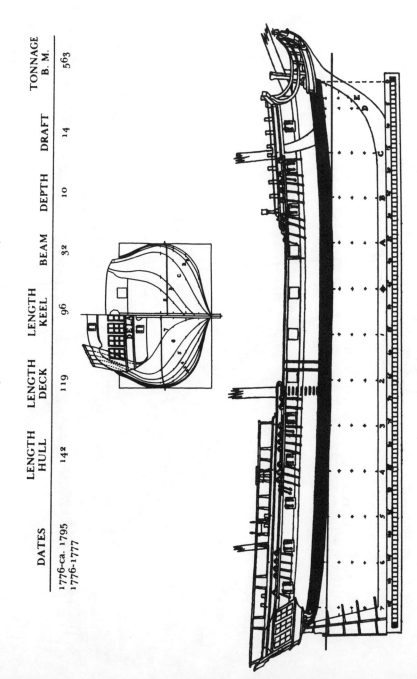

WARREN (ex-AMERICA), 32

(conjectural reconstruction)

DATES	LENGTH HULL	LENGTH DECK	LENGTH KEEL	BEAM	DEPTH	DRAFT	TONNAGE B. M.
1776-1779	152	132	111	34	11	17	690

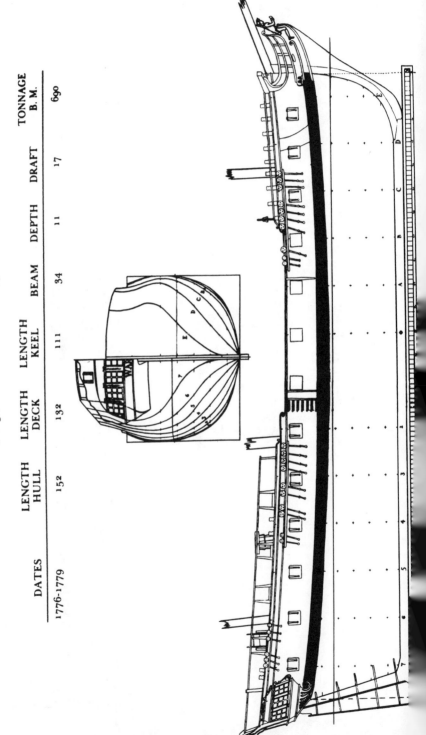

(conjectural reconstruction)

DATES	LENGTH HULL	LENGTH DECK	LENGTH KEEL	BEAM	DEPTH	DRAFT	TONNAGE B. M.
1776-?	144	124	103	34	10	16	632

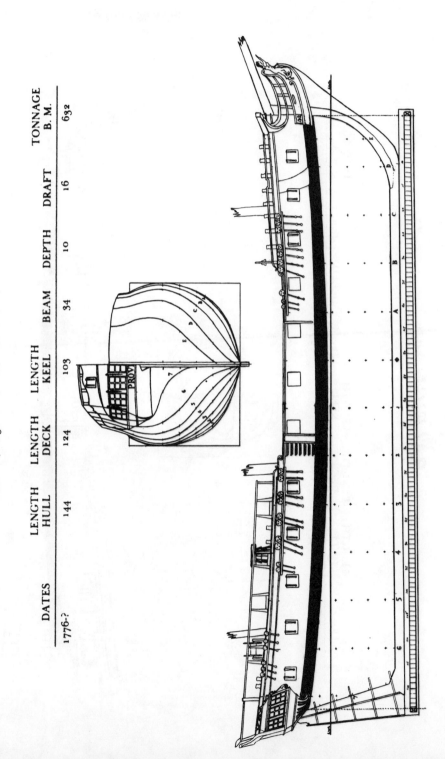

RALEIGH, 32

DATES	LENGTH HULL	LENGTH DECK	LENGTH KEEL	BEAM	DEPTH	DRAFT	TONNAGE B. M.
1776-?	154	131	111	34	11	17	697

DATES	LENGTH HULL	LENGTH DECK	LENGTH KEEL	BEAM	DEPTH	DRAFT	TONNAGE B. M.
1776-1793	162	137	116	35	11	17	762

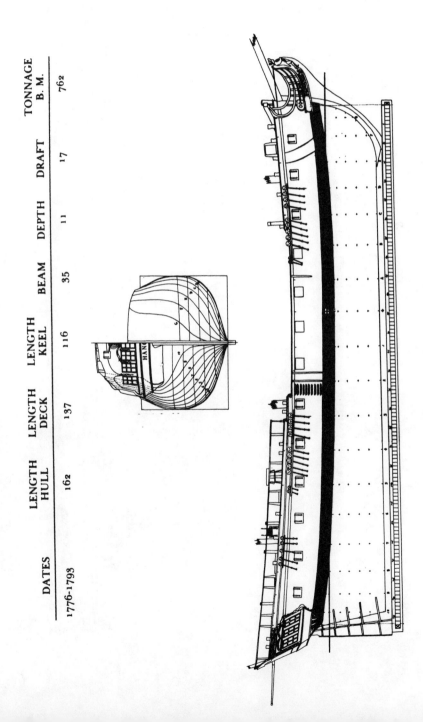

BOSTON, 24

(conjectural reconstruction)

DATES	LENGTH HULL	LENGTH DECK	LENGTH KEEL	BEAM	DEPTH	DRAFT	TONNAGE B. M.
1776-?	139	114	93	32	10	14	514

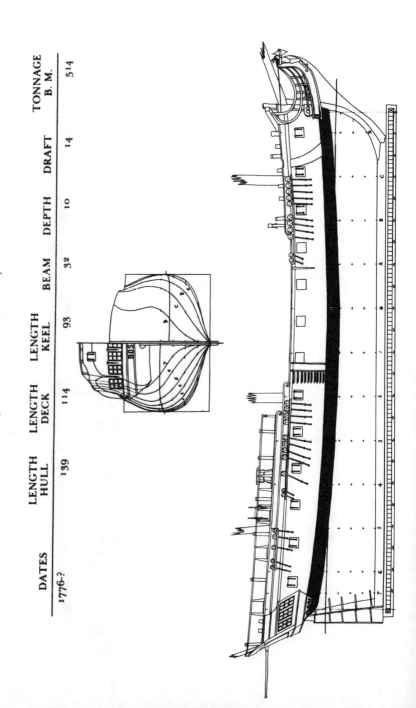

QUEEN OF FRANCE (*ex-LA BRUNE*), 28

(conjectural reconstruction)

DATES	LENGTH HULL	LENGTH DECK	LENGTH KEEL	BEAM	DEPTH	DRAFT	TONNAGE B. M.
ca. 1757–1780	ESTIMATED 137	118	98	34	15	17	581

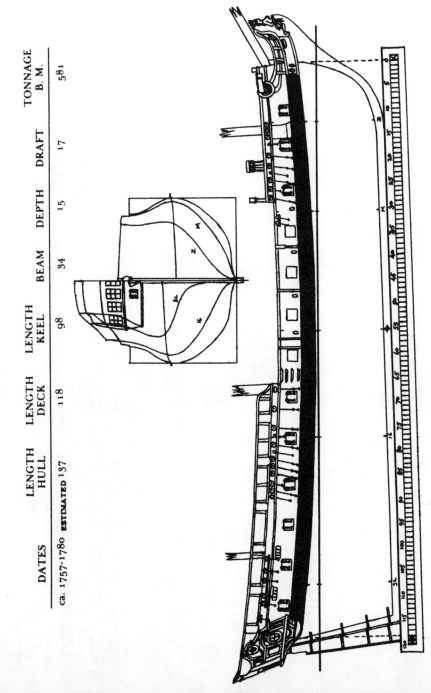

DEANE/HAGUE, 32

(conjectural reconstruction)

DATES	LENGTH HULL	LENGTH DECK	LENGTH KEEL	BEAM	DEPTH	DRAFT	TONNAGE B. M.
1777-?	136	117	96	32	10	15	517

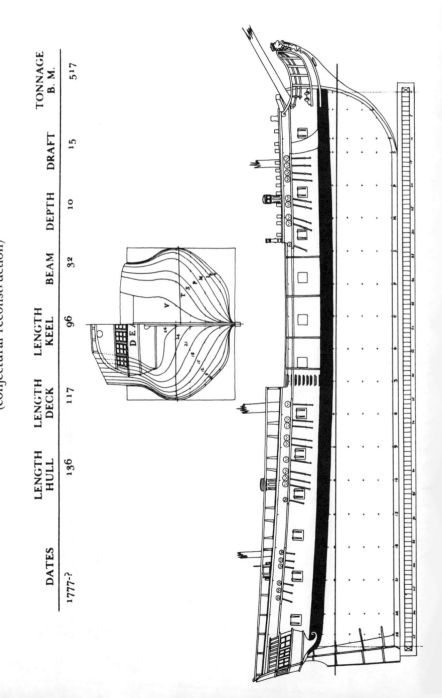

CONFEDERACY, BOURBON & [un-named], 36

DATES	LENGTH HULL	LENGTH DECK	LENGTH KEEL	BEAM	DEPTH	DRAFT	TONNAGE B. M.
1778-1782 178?-? 1779-1779	185	155	133	37	12	16	971

ALLIANCE *(ex-JOHN HANCOCK), 36*

(conjectural reconstruction)

DATES	LENGTH HULL	LENGTH DECK	LENGTH KEEL	BEAM	DEPTH	DRAFT	TONNAGE B. M.
1777-1800	178	151	180	36	13	17	910

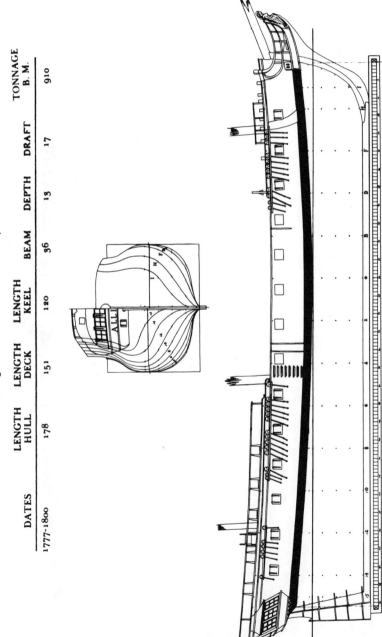

SOUTH CAROLINA (ex-L'INDIEN), 40

DATES	LENGTH HULL	LENGTH DECK	LENGTH KEEL	BEAM	DEPTH	DRAFT	TONNAGE B. M.
1777-1782	198	164	147	44	18	23	1430

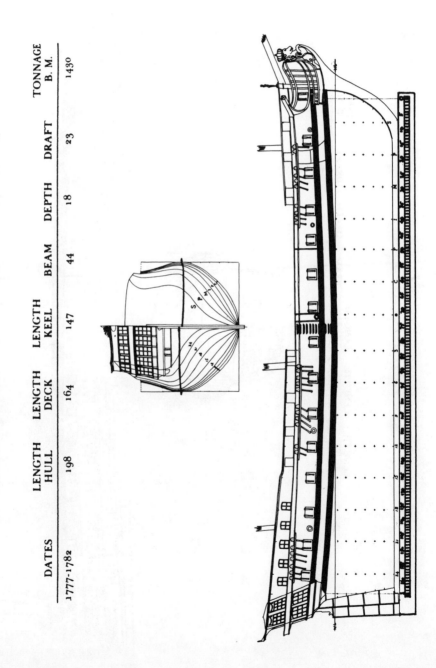

AMERICA, 74

DATES	LENGTH HULL	LENGTH DECK	LENGTH KEEL	BEAM	DEPTH	DRAFT	TONNAGE B. M.
1777-1786	221	180	147	49	19	24	1982

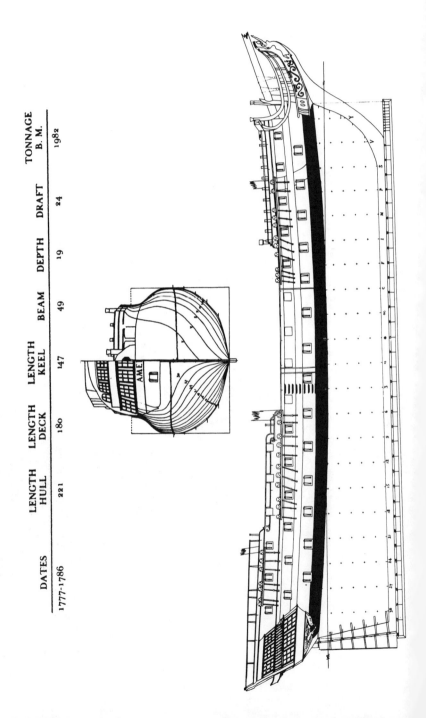

SARATOGA, 16

DATES

1777-1781

LENGTH HULL	LENGTH DECK	LENGTH KEEL	BEAM	DEPTH	DRAFT	TONNAGE B. M.
100	85	68	25	13	13	240

(conjectural reconstruction)

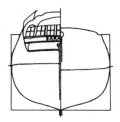

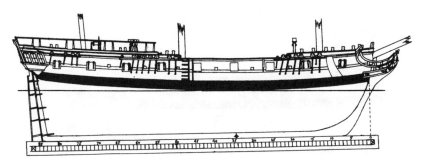

GENERAL WASHINGTON 20

DATES

1779-ca. 1794

LENGTH HULL	LENGTH DECK	LENGTH KEEL	BEAM	DEPTH	DRAFT	TONNAGE B. M.
ESTIMATED 117	98	81	30	14	14	340

(conjectural reconstruction)

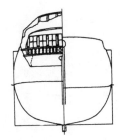

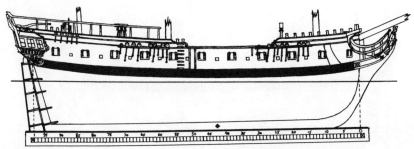

RANGER (ex-HAMPSHIRE) 18

| | | | | | | DATES |
| | | | | | | 1777-1781 |

LENGTH HULL	LENGTH DECK	LENGTH KEEL	BEAM	DEPTH	DRAFT	TONNAGE B. M.
116	97	82	29	13	12	308

(conjectural reconstruction)

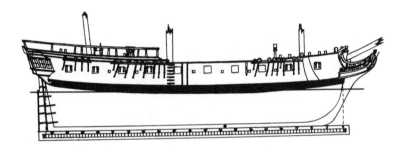

HERO (ex-GENERAL GATES) 18

| | | | | | | DATES |
| | | | | | | 1777-1777 |

LENGTH HULL	LENGTH DECK	LENGTH KEEL	BEAM	DEPTH	DRAFT	TONNAGE B. M.
ESTIMATED 111	94	80	27	11	12	300

(conjectural reconstruction)

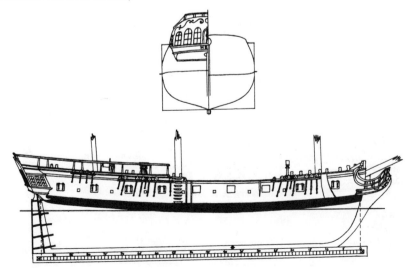

BONHOMME RICHARD (ex-DUC DE DURAS), 42

DATES	LENGTH HULL	LENGTH DECK	LENGTH KEEL	BEAM	DEPTH	DRAFT	TONNAGE B. M.
55-1779	188	155	135	39	16	19	1050

njectural reconstruction)

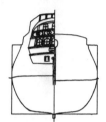

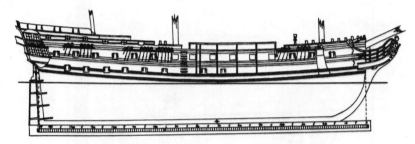

PROVIDENCE (ex-KATY), 12

ATES	LENGTH HULL	LENGTH DECK	LENGTH KEEL	BEAM	DEPTH	DRAFT	TONNAGE B. M.
9-1779	67	59	49	20	7	9	95
ESTIMATED							

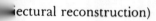

iectural reconstruction)

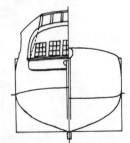

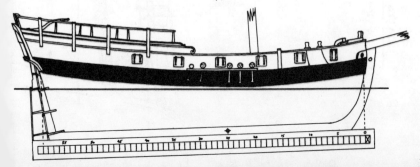

OLIVER CROMWELL, 16

DATES	LENGTH HULL	LENGTH DECK	LENGTH KEEL	BEAM	DEPTH	DRAFT	TONNAGE B. M.
ca. 1774-1780	102	86	69	26	12	13	248

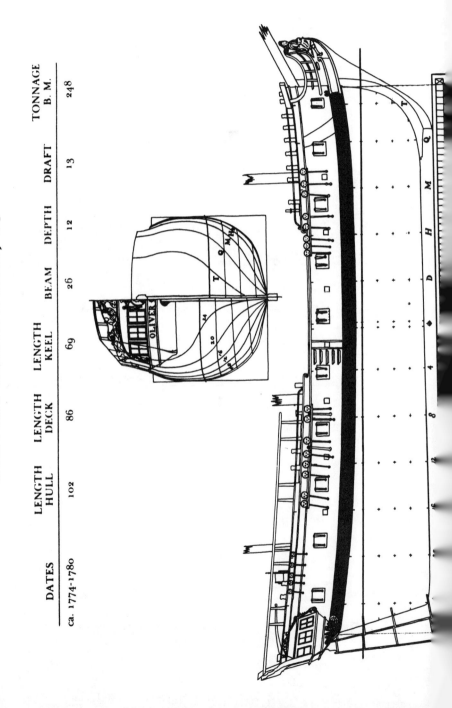

Color of topside planking of typical eighteenth-century warships.

JOURNAL
OF THE COMMITTEE WHO BUILT
THE SHIPS
PROVIDENCE AND *WARREN*
FOR THE UNITED STATES
AD 1776

Providence, January 8, 1776

At a meeting of the committee appointed to build two ships for the service of the Continent of America.

Present: Honble. Nicholas Cooke Esq.
                 Nicholas Brown
                 Joseph Russell
                 Joseph Brown
                 John Brown
                 John Smith
                 William Russell
                 Daniel Tillinghast
                 John Innes Clark
                 Joseph Nightingale
                 Jabez Bowen[1]

Voted: That the Honorable Nicholas Cooke Esq. be chairman of this committee, and Henry Ward Esq. clerk.

Voted: That Jabez Bowen be clerk *pro tempore.*

Whereas there is a quantity of ship timber now

at Pawtucket landing, 'tis voted that Jonathan
Jenckes Esq. be employed to go to the people
that own the same and purchase it on the best
terms he can, and that he get as much of it to
be delivered in town as possible. The remainder he is to get carted as soon as practicable
and on as reasonable terms as may be, that he
purchase one hundred tons of timber more to
consist mostly of floor and rising timber and
plank logs on the best terms he can, to be
delivered in Providence immediately.

Voted: That Captain Barnard Eddy be employed to
get the keel, stem, stern post, and transom for
the largest of the ships, and that he procure
the same to be carted as soon as possible, that
he agree for the said timber on the most
reasonable terms he can, and that he take as
many good carpenters and axmen as he may
think he can employ to advantage, and also
that he get any other kind of timber that may
be wanted for the building the said ships.

Voted: That Captain Nicholas Power[2] go to Newport
and engage all the pine timber that will do to
saw into plank and all the spars and plank that
will answer for the ships, that he engage all the
ship carpenters in Warren and Newport, also
that he procure as much locust for treenails as
he can, that he endeavor to get Major Benjamin Tallman[3] to leave the service to engage in
building the ships, and that he procure some
proper person to get the timber and spars
brought off the island as soon as possible, that
he call on Mr. Langley and purchase the
boards he has now in this town, and that he

engage all the naval stores that are to be sold in Newport.

Voted: That Colonel William Russell go to Warren and engage Mr. Moses Tyler, or any other suitable person, to come to Providence for a master builder to carry on one of the ships, also that he go to Swansea and engage all the carpenters and plank he can.

Voted: That there be 25,000 feet plank of 2½ inches engaged as soon as may be.

Voted: That the running plank under the wale be four inches thick.

Reckoning: 12/- L My paid by John Brown.

Meeting adjourned to tomorrow evening, 6 o'clock, this place.

****

January 9, 1776

Meeting in being according to adjournment.

Present: Honble. Nicholas Cooke Esq.
              Nicholas Brown
              Joseph Brown
              John Brown
              John Smith
              Joseph Nightingale
              John I. Clark
              Rufus Hopkins
              Jabez Bowen

Voted: That Mr. John Smith procure all the ship carpenters, ship timber, and plank he possibly can, and that he employ a proper person to go to Marshfield etc. to engage what carpenters are out of employ there.

Voted: That Captains Christopher Sheldon and Pardon Sheldon[4] be appointed clerks to take an account of all the timber, plank, iron, etc. that shall be brought into the shipyard, and that Nicholas Brown, Joseph Nightingale, and Jabez Bowen be a committee to agree with them for their wages, and also that they agree with Christopher Sheldon, Thurber's, Cahoon's, Captain Joseph Tillinghast,[5] John Aplin's guardians, [and] Mr. Ebenezer Thompson for the lands that may be wanted to build the ships on and lay the timber.

Voted: That Joseph Brown and John I. Clark be appointed a committee to agree with Messrs. Joseph and Daniel Bucklin[6] on the terms that they will undertake the blockmakers' bills for the ships.

Voted: That Mr. John Brown and Joseph Nightingale be a committee to inquire on what terms the blacksmiths' work can be done for the ships.

Voted: That Jabez Bowen and John I. Clark be a committee to agree with the boat builders for the boats that may be wanted for the ships.

Voted: That eighteen shillings per ton be given for all ship timber that will measuré 12 inches square at the top end and to be 40 feet in length, and 20/- per ton if 45 feet long and 12 inches at top, and 15/- for all timber that shall be 12 inches square and 25 feet long, and 16/- for 30 feet long, and 17/- for 35 feet long.

Memorandum: Messrs. Brown and Power agree to furnish the rigging for one of the ships, certain, and as much more as they can make for the other @ 54/- per hundred.

Voted: That Messrs. Clark and Nightingale send for

ten tons of sterling bar iron to New York for the use of the ships at the risque of the Continent.

Reckoning: 12/- L My paid by John Brown. [L My=Lawful Money]

Meeting adjourned to tomorrow evening, 6 o'clock.

****

January 10, 1776

Meeting in being according to adjournment.

Present: Honble. Nicholas Cooke Esq.
Nicholas Brown
Joseph Brown
John Brown
Joseph Russell
Rufus Hopkins
John I. Clark
Joseph Nightingale
Jabez Bowen

Voted: That Mr. Moses Tyler be desired to go to Cambridge and the neighboring towns and engage all the good ship carpenters he can to come here to work on the ships, that he offer 4/6 per day, they boarding themselves, and that he be allowed a reasonable sum for his time and expenses for doing the said business. For master workmen a higher price will be given.

Voted: That Mr. Sylvester Bowers[7] make a draught of the largest ship as soon as may be.

Reckoning: 22/- L My paid by Joseph Nightingale.

Meeting adjourned to Friday evening, 6 o'clock.

****

January 12, 1776

Meeting in being according to adjournment.
Present: Honble. Nicholas Cooke Esq.
                 Joseph Russell
                 Nicholas Brown
                 Joseph Brown
                 John Brown
                 Joseph Nightingale
                 John I. Clark
                 William Russell
                 John Smith
                 Jabez Bowen
Voted: That John Brown, John Smith, and William
             Russell be a committee to agree with the ship
             carpenters for the wages they shall receive for
             working on the ships, that they send them out
             to the different farms to cut timber immediate-
             ly, and that they provide places for them to
             board in when they shall arrive in town. Meet-
             ing adjourned to Saturday evening at 6 o'clock.
Reckoning: 12/- L My paid by Joseph Nightingale.
                      ****

January 13, 1776

Meeting in being according to adjournment.
Present: Joseph Brown
                 John Brown
                 Daniel Tillinghast
                 William Russell
                 Jabez Bowen
                 John I. Clark
                 Joseph Nightingale
                 Nicholas Brown
                 John Smith

Voted: That Jonathan Jenckes Esq. send plank logs to Kent's and Atherton's sawmills, and that he have them sawed into 4 inch plank and as long as the mills will admit, and that he provide two sawpits and set proper men to work in them constantly in sawing 4 inch plank at Pawtucket landing, and that he agree with mill and pit sawyers for the price of sawing, that the same persons that bring the logs to the mill are to engage to bring the plank to town.

Reckoning: 11/- L My paid by Col. Nightingale

****

Monday evening January 15, 1776

Meeting in being according to adjournment.

Present: Joseph Brown, chosen chairman
Nicholas Brown
John Brown
Daniel Tillinghast
William Russell
John I. Clark
Jabez Bowen
Joseph Nightingale

Voted: That Nicholas Brown and Captain Nicholas Power write to Mr. George Scott to procure and deliver 30 tons of locusts (for treenails) at Bristol Ferry wharf on the island side, and that the customary price for the same be 42/- per ton.

Voted: That there be 2 dozen treenail augers of 1½ inch, fifteen of 1¼ inch, 12 of 1 inch for scarfing the keel, deck, etc., six of 1 1/8 inch for floor timber bolts, six [of] 7/8 inch, six of 3/4 inch, that William Russell send John Cruger of Uxbridge for them.

Voted: That there be 4 streaks of 4½ inch plank at the
          ring heads, one streak under and one over the
          wale 5 inches, and that the main deck plank be
          4 inches thick, the quarterdeck and forecastle
          plank be 3 inches thick, sealing, 5 inch plank
          for the ringhead and 4 plank wide, two streaks
          for the clamps, 6½ inch thick, all the rest two
          inch plank double.

Voted: That Mr. Caleb Bowers procure two main-
          masts of 86 feet long and 26 inches diameter
          and two foremasts 78 feet long and 23 inches
          diameter for the ships on the best terms he
          can, that he also purchase at [   ], 9000 feet of 3
          inch pine plank to be delivered here on the
          best terms he can, and that they be as long as
          possible.

Voted: That there be three wales 8 inches thick, the
          middle one 8½ inches, the waist and sealing
          for the same from 4 to 2½ inches thick, the
          floor timbers 17 inches deep at the throat and
          12 inches at the surmark, sided 11 inches, that
          she diminish from the surmark to the wale 9
          inches at the top timber heads to 6 inches,
          length of floor timbers 17 feet from surmark to
          surmark and 18 inches head, dead rising 20
          inches.

          Dimensions of the 32 gun ship
          gundeck 132 feet 1 inch
          keel ....110....10 3/4.
          beam ....34....5½....
          hold....11.....
          Dimensions 28 gun ship
          gundeck 124 feet 4 inches
          keel ....102....8½....

beam ....33.....10 3/8...
hold ....10....8.....
Reckoning: 20/- L My paid by Col Nightingale.
Meeting adjourned to tomorrow evening, 6
o'clock.

****

January 16, 1776

Meeting in being according to adjournment.
Present: Joseph Russell
Nicholas Brown
Joseph Brown
William Russell
John I. Clark
Joseph Nightingale
Jabez Bowen
John Brown
Reckoning: 10/- L My paid by Joseph Nightingale.
Meeting adjourned to tomorrow evening, 6
o'clock.

****

January 17, 1776

Meeting in being according to adjournment.
Present: Honble. Nicholas Cooke Esq.
Nicholas Brown
Joseph Brown
John Brown
William Russell
Daniel Tillinghast
John I. Clark
Joseph Nightingale
Jabez Bowen

Sundry matters were negotiated this evening for the forwarding the business.

Reckoning: 21/- L My paid by Joseph Nightingale.

Meeting adjourned to Friday evening, 6 o'clock.

****

January 19, 1776

Meeting in being according to adjournment.

Present: Honble. Nicholas Cooke Esq.

Nicholas Brown

Joseph Russell

Joseph Brown

John Smith

Daniel Tillinghast

John Brown

John I. Clark

Joseph Nightingale

Jabez Bowen

William Russell

Voted: That Benjamin Tallman be master carpenter for the largest ship.

Voted: That Mr. John I. Clark go to Newport tomorrow to purchase all the cordage he can not exceeding 20 tons at not exceeding nine dollars p/c, also to hurry the spars and pine logs to be got up as fast as possible, to buy all the good bar iron he can, to call on James Daggett on his way and engage him to get all the timber and plank he can, to dispatch the locust as soon as may be, to get what 2d, 3d, 4d, 6d, 8d, 10d, and 20d nails he can, get all the clear pine boards and plank he can and make up the qt. with merchantable to 20 m. feet, and as many of them in plank as he can, to engage what iron hoops can be had in Newport @ 40/- p/c and what white oak hhd. staves he can @ 20 dollars p/c, d/d in Providence, to purchase codlines, pump and scupper nails, and English augers of 1 and 1 1/8 inch, to call on John Manley[8] what he has done respecting the spars and purchase all Miller has.

Voted: That Nicholas Brown Esq. be treasurer and paymaster to this committee.

Voted: That Nicholas Cooke Jr. and Joseph [Dolbear] Russell Jr.[9] go to Philadelphia and bring sixty thousand dollars at least and as much more as Mr. [Stephen] Hopkins shall think proper to send by them, and that they be allowed six shillings per day and twenty dollars each for their horses and their reasonable expenses.

Voted: That Nicholas Brown, William Russell, and Jabez Bowen write a letter to the Honble. Stephen Hopkins Esq. to send by the above young gentlemen, and that the same be signed by a majority of this committee.[10]

Reckoning: 22/6 paid by Col Nightingale.

Meeting adjourned to Monday evening, 6 o'clock.

****

January 22, 1776

Meeting in being according to adjournment.

Present: Honble. Nicholas Cooke Esq.
            Nicholas Brown
            Joseph Russell
            Joseph Brown
            Daniel Tillinghast

John Brown
John Smith
William Russell
Joseph Nightingale
Jabez Bowen

Voted: That thirteen pounds 10/- L My for good
           sound four inch plank of thirty feet long and
           upwards.

Voted: That good sound square plank logs of 30 feet
           long and upwards and well hewed be 20/- per
           ton delivered in town.

Voted: That Sylvester Bowers be master workman for
           the smallest of the ships.

Reckoning: 22/6 paid by Col Nightingale.

           Meeting adjourned to Wednesday night, 6
           o'clock.

                    ****

                                      January 24, 1776

           Meeting in being according to adjournment.

Present: Honble. Nicholas Cooke Esq.
           Nicholas Brown
           Joseph Russell
           Joseph Brown
           Daniel Tillinghast
           William Russell
           John I. Clark
           Joseph Nightingale
           Jabez Bowen

Voted: That the board of the carpenters from abroad
           be paid in stormy weather when they are not
           able to work. Whereas Henry Ward Esq. who
           was chosen secretary to this committee cannot
           give his attendance on the said committee

meetings from the multiplicity of public business that he has to transact, it is voted that Jabez Bowen be chosen secretary to this committee.

Reckoning: 22/6 paid by Col. Nightingale.

Meeting adjourned to Friday evening, 6 o'clock.

****

January 26, 1776

Meeting in being according to adjournment.

Present: Honble. Nicholas Cooke Esq.
Nicholas Brown
Joseph Brown
Daniel Tillinghast
John Brown
John I. Clark
Joseph Nightingale
William Russell
Jabez Bowen

Reckoning: 16/6 paid by Col. Nightingale.

Meeting adjourned to Monday night, 6 o'clock.

****

January 29, 1776

Meeting in being according to adjournment.

Present: Honble. Nicholas Cooke Esq.
Nicholas Brown
Joseph Brown
Rufus Hopkins
John Brown
Daniel Tillinghast
John Smith
William Russell

John I. Clark

Jabez Bowen

Voted: That Mr. Elkanah Palmer be employed to get the four masts for the ships (in the room of Mr. Caleb Bowers), and that he proceed to get the sticks cut and transported by land to Providence if possible; if not, then to have them brought to Wrentham; if it cannot be done to either of the above places, then to get them to Taunton on the best terms he can, that he also get two bowsprits, the one to be 52 feet long, 25 inches diameter, the other to be 48 feet long and 23 inches diameter, to be transported in the same manner as the masts.

N.B. The masts are to be procured according to the dimensions given to Mr. Bowers.

Voted: That Mr. George Olney[11] be employed as clerk to keep the books of accounts necessary in the building of the ships and to transact any other business the committee may employ him about, that he have six pounds twelve shillings per month for said service, he to board himself in the neighborhood and give constant attendance till the business be done in the evening.

Reckoning: 23/- paid by Col. Nightingale.

Meeting adjourned to Wednesday evening, 6 o'clock.

****

January 31, 1776

Meeting in being according to adjournment.

Present: Honble. Nicholas Cooke Esq.

Nicholas Brown

Henry Ward

Joseph Brown

Daniel Tillinghast
John Brown
Joseph Nightingale
William Russell
Jabez Bowen
Voted: That Mr. John I. Clark engage twenty tons of hemp at Salem provided it may be delivered here for 54/- p/c.
Voted: That this committee approve of Mr. Nicholas Brown's advancing thirty pounds L My to Mr. Elkanah Palmer to enable him to procure the masts for the ships.
Reckoning: 21/- paid by Col Nightingale.
Meeting adjourned to Friday evening, 6 o'clock.

****

February 2, 1776

Meeting in being according to adjournment.
Present: Honble. Nicholas Cooke Esq.
Nicholas Brown
Daniel Tillinghast
John Brown
William Russell
Joseph Nightingale
Reckoning: 7/6 paid by Col. Nightingale.
Meeting adjourned to Monday evening, 6 o'clock.

****

February 5, 1776

Meeting in being according to adjournment.
Present: Honble. Nicholas Cooke Esq.
Nicholas Brown
Daniel Tillinghast

Joseph Brown
Joseph Nightingale
John I. Clark
William Russell
Henry Ward
Jabez Bowen
Gave a draught to Mr. John Brown on Stephen Hopkins Esq. for five thousand dollars.
Also gave a draught to Welcome Arnold Esq.[12] on Stephen Hopkins Esq. for one thousand dollars.
Agreed with Cromwell Child for 8000 feet of 2½ inch plank to be d/d here on demand for twenty-five dollars per thousand.

Voted: That Messrs. Clark and Nightingale write to Mr. Frank Brindley to engage twenty tons of rigging of him on the terms he offered afore, that is ten dollars per hundred at the rope walk to be made up as soon as possible and of such sizes as the committee shall direct.

Reckoning: 18/- paid by Col. Nightingale.
Meeting adjourned to Wednesday evening, 6 o'clock.

****

February 7, 1776

Meeting in being according to adjournment.
Present: Honble. Nicholas Cooke Esq.
Nicholas Brown
Joseph Russell
Joseph Brown
John Brown
Daniel Tillinghast

Joseph Nightingale
John I. Clark
John Smith
William Russell
Jabez Bowen

Voted: That Captain Charles Jenckes be employed to get all the bar iron, timber, boards, naval stores, etc. now brought or to be brought from Newport to Fogland Ferry to be shipped up here as soon as possible, and that Mr. Gladding bring all the locust and spars from Bristol Ferry, and are accordingly to be written to for this purpose.

Voted: That 400 good firearms, 400 good pistols, 40 swivel guns, and 400 cutlasses be procured by Messrs. Clark and Nightingale as soon as may be at the risque of the Continent.

Voted: That Mr. Joseph Russell go to Attleboro tomorrow to hurry the timber in as fast as possible, that Mr. John Smith go to Cumberland for the same purpose, and that Mr. Daniel Tillinghast go to North Providence and Smithfield, and Mr. Benoni Pierce go to Cranston and Johnston for the same purpose, that 10/- per ton be given for carting all common timber from 8 to 9 miles distance and 7/- per ton be given from 4½ to 6 miles distance and that a further reasonable allowance be made for the carting of all crooked or bad timber or for getting it out from bad or difficult places.

Reckoning: 22/6 paid by [ ]

Meeting adjourned to Friday evening, 6 o'clock.

****

February 9, 1776

Meeting in being according to adjournment.

Present: Honble. Nicholas Cooke Esq.
Nicholas Brown
Joseph Russell
William Russell
Joseph Nightingale
Daniel Tillinghast
John I. Clark
Joseph Brown
Jabez Bowen

Voted: That a letter be written to William Ellery Esq.[13] desiring him to meet Governor Cooke at Warren on Monday next at 12 o'clock if a fair day, if not, then the next fair day, in order to purchase the iron, rigging, etc. that belong to Mr. Levey which is under attachment there, and that Jabez Bowen write the letter.

Reckoning: 17/- paid by
Meeting adjourned to Monday next.
****

February 12, 1776

Meeting in being according to adjournment.

Present: Nicholas Brown
Joseph Brown
Daniel Tillinghast
Joseph Nightingale
William Russell
John I. Clark
Jabez Bowen
John Brown, chairman for the evening

Voted: That Col. William Russell, Mr. Sylvester Bowers, and Major Tallman give lists of the names of all the carpenters that are at work in the shipyards, and that they affix the prices that each man is to have per day according to their several abilities as workmen, and make report to the next meeting.

Voted: That Messrs. Clark and Nightingale deliver nine tons of pig iron to Thomas Arnold,[14] Daniel Thornton, and James Appleby Jr. on the account on risque of the Continent.

Voted: That Mr. Manley agree with Mr. Lee for all the spars he has on hand on the best terms he can.

Voted: That Mr. John Brown write a letter to Mr. Hezekiah Sabin,[15] merchant in New Haven, and request him to purchase for the use of the Continental ships two hundred and fifty barrels of pork and one hundred and fifty barrels of beef, the price of the pork to be at 54/- and the beef @ 40/- per Bbl. at New Haven, that if it cannot be procured at the above prices, that he write to Mr. John Brown on the same subject immediately, that he be allowed two and a half percent for doing the business, and that Mr. John Brown draw on Messrs. Joseph Dolbear Russell and Nicholas Cooke Jr. to pay to the said Mr. Hezekiah Sabin the sum of three thousand five hundred dollars to pay for the same, and that he purchase two hundred bushels of beans and peas, that a majority of the committee sign the order.

Voted: That we send a messenger to [Chatham], Connecticut to procure a draught of the ship to be built there immediately.

Reckoning: 28/6 paid by [   ]
Meeting adjourned to Wednesday evening, 6
o'clock.
****
February 14, 1776

Meeting in being according to adjournment.
Reckoning: 28/6 paid by [   ]
Meeting adjourned to Wednesday evening, 6
o'clock,
****
February 14, 1776

Meeting in being according to adjournment.
Reckoning: 20/- [   ]
Meeting adjourned to Friday evening.
****
February 16, 1776

Meeting in being according to adjournment.
Present: Honble. Nicholas Cooke Esq.
Nicholas Brown
Joseph Brown
John Brown
Daniel Tillinghast
Joseph Nightingale
John I. Clark
William Russell
Jabez Bowen
Reckoning: 17/-
Meeting adjourned to Monday evening.
****
February 19, 1776

Meeting in being according to adjournment.
Present: Honble. Nicholas Cooke Esq.

Nicholas Brown
Joseph Brown
John Brown
Daniel Tillinghast
John Smith
Joseph Nightingale
William Russell
John I. Clark
Joseph Russell
Jabez Bowen

Messrs. Joseph D. Russell and Nicholas Cooke Jr. having returned last evening from Philadelphia, made their appearance this evening to report their doings to the committee. They have brought the sixty thousand dollars in cash sent for by this committee; they have also brought the draughts of the two ships which we were desired to build for the Continental service, and on examining the same, we find it impossible to follow the draughts sent us without retarding the work at least one month. On considering the whole matter, it is voted that Messrs. Bowers and Tallman proceed to finish the bottoms of the ships according to their present molds, and that they finish the upper works nearly according to the directions sent us by Stephen Hopkins Esq., tumbling the sides home two feet on each side.

Whereas Nicholas Brown Esq. was heretofore chosen treasurer to this committee, and he making sundry excuses which rendered it inconvenient for him to execute the said trust, the matter was determined by lot when it fell on Mr. John I. Clark to execute the said trust, and Messrs. Russell and Cooke Jr. are hereby ordered to pay the money to the said Mr. Clark.

Voted: That the sum of fifty seven pounds nine shillings and eight pence lawful money be paid to Nicholas Cooke Jr. and Joseph D. Russell for their expenses to Philadelphia on the business of this committee.

Voted: That Mr. John Brown write Mr. Hezekiah Sabin of New Haven and request him to purchase two hundred barrels of flour for this committee, and that Mr. John I. Clark, the treasurer, pay to Mr. Hezekiah Sabin Jr. who will soon be in this town the sum of four thousand five hundred dollars to purchase beef, pork, beans, and flour, and that he purchase the above articles on the best terms he can.

Voted: That this committee approve the order on Stephen Hopkins Esq. in favor of Nicholas Brown Esq. and John Brown for three thousand dollars, dated the 17th of this instant.

Reckoning: 29/-

Meeting adjourned to Wednesday evening.

****

February 21, 1776

Meeting in being according to adjournment.

Present: Honble. Nicholas Cooke Esq.
           Nicholas Brown
           Joseph Russell
           Joseph Brown
           Daniel Tillinghast
           Joseph Nightingale

John I. Clark
William Russell
Jabez Bowen

Voted: That the sum of two hundred ninety-two pounds twelve shillings and six pence one farthing L My be paid Messrs Brown and Power out of the committee's treasury.

Voted: That Messrs. Joseph and William Russell's account amounting to one hundred and eleven pounds eleven shillings and six pence lawful money be paid out of the committee's treasury. Agreed with Nathanael Greene and Company [16] for the anchors for the small ship @ 8d per lb. as per agreement on file.

Voted: That the sum of seven hundred sixty-four pounds four shillings and eight pence L My, being the balance of John Brown's account, be paid him out of the committee's treasury.

Reckoning: 33/-

Meeting adjourned to Friday evening.

****

February 23, 1776

Meeting in being according to adjournment.

Present: Honble. Nicholas Cooke Esq.
Nicholas Brown
Joseph Brown
John Brown
William Russell
John I. Clark
Jabez Bowen
Joseph Nightingale

Voted: That a bill for two thousand dollars be drawn on Stephen Hopkins Esq. in favor of Captain

Caleb Gardner on his paying the amount into
the hands of John I. Clark, the treasurer.

Voted: That a bill for eight hundred dollars be drawn
on Stephen Hopkins Esq. in favor of Peter T.
Curtenius to purchase bar iron for the use of
the ships.

N.B.   The committee has written to Mr. P. T. Curtenius to procure two anchors 30 C wt. each for
the ships at 9d York My per lb.

Reckoning: [   ]

Meeting adjourned to Monday evening.
****

February 26, 1776

Meeting in being according to adjournment.

Present: Nicholas Brown chairman
Joseph Russell
Joseph Brown
Daniel Tillinghast
John Brown
Joseph Nightingale
John I. Clark
William Russell
Jabez Bowen

Voted: That forty-eight pieces of English duck be
purchased of H. A. Lopez at the following
prices: 29 of No. 1 @ £6; 5 of No. 2, £5 17/-; 9
of No. 3, £5 14/-; 5 of No.5, £5 8/-.

Voted: That the sum of two hundred sixty-two
pounds six shillings and four pence three
farthings be paid Messrs. Brown and Power
out of the committee's treasury.

Voted: That the sum of five hundred forty-four
pounds seven shillings and five pence three

farthings be paid Nicholas Brown out of the committee's treasury.

Voted: That Joseph Nightingale be appointed to agree for a Vessel to go to New Haven to bring a load of provisions on the best terms he can.

Reckoning: 20/-

Meeting adjourned to Wednesday evening.

****

February 28, 1776

Meeting in being according to adjournment.

Present: Nicholas Brown
Joseph Russell
Joseph Brown
Joseph Nightingale
John Brown

Gave Mr. Palmer a memorandum to get two spars 73 feet long, to work 18 inches in the slings, one spar for mizzenmast 72 feet long, 16½ inches in the partners, one ditto for ditto 69 feet long, 16½ inches in the partners, all the above to be transported to the nearest water carriage and then rafted to Taunton.

Voted: That the treasurer pay Mr. Elkanah Palmer seventy pounds lawful money towards procuring the masts and spars according to orders.

Reckoning: 22/6

Meeting adjourned to Friday evening.

****

March 1, 1776

Meeting in being according to adjournment.

Present: Nicholas Brown
Joseph Russell

Joseph Brown
John Brown
Daniel Tillinghast
Joseph Nightingale
John I. Clark
William Russell
Jabez Bowen

Voted: That Mr. Barnard Eddy go into the country and cut and send in all the knees he possibly can, on the best terms he possibly can, that he also engage carters to bring in the timber from Tyler's lot on the best terms he can, he observing to make written agreements with all the people he may employ.

Voted: That Captain Pardon Sheldon take a list of all the carpenters in Bowers' yard, that he call the list at sunrise and sunset, and to make return to the committee's clerk every Saturday before the time of paying the men off.

Voted: That Captain Christopher Sheldon take a list of the carpenters in Major Tallman's yard and call the list and make return as above.

That 25 dollars be given for all 3 inch plank delivered in the yard by the middle of March.

Voted: That one of the committee attend the shipyards constantly, and that it be by lot, which fell as follows: Nicholas Brown to attend on Monday; John I. Clark, Tuesday; Daniel Tillinghast, Wednesday; William Russell, Thursday; Joseph Russell, Friday; John Brown, Saturday; John Smith, Monday 2nd; Joseph Nightingale, Tuesday 2nd; Jabez Bowen, 2nd Wednesday.

Gave Mr. Jones an order on the treasurer for £12. 16. 6. in full to this 1st March inclusive.

Reckoning: 28/6

Meeting adjourned to Monday evening.
****

March 4, 1776

Meeting in being according to adjournment.

Present: Honble. Nicholas Cooke Esq.
Nicholas Brown
Daniel Tillinghast
Joseph Nightingale
John I. Clark
William Russell
Joseph Brown
John Brown
Jabez Bowen

Voted: That the committee's treasurer pay Mr. Cromwell Child one hundred and twenty pounds lawful money in part pay for timber and iron bought of him.

Voted: That the sum of twenty-four pounds seven shillings and eleven pence ½d be paid to Jabez Bowen out of the committee's treasury, being the amount of his account.

Voted: That the sum of one hundred and ninety-eight pounds eleven shillings be paid Mr. John Brown out of the committee's treasury, it being for duck bought of him.

:ckoning: [ ]

Meeting adjourned to Wednesday evening.
****

Wednesday evening March 6, 1776

Meeting in being according to adjournment.

Present: Honble. Nicholas Cooke Esq.
Nicholas Brown

> Joseph Brown
> John Smith
> Henry Ward
> John I. Clark
> Jabez Bowen

Voted: That the sum of one hundred and ninety-
          seven pounds three shillings and two pence
          ½d be paid to Mr. John Smith out of the
          committee's treasury, being the amount of his
          account.

Reckoning: [   ]

          Meeting adjourned to Friday evening.
                    ****

                              Friday evening March 8, 1776

          Meeting in being according to adjournment.

Present: Honble. Nicholas Cooke Esq.
                   Nicholas Brown
                   Joseph Russell
                   Joseph Brown
                   Joseph Nightingale
                   John I. Clark
                   Jabez Bowen

Voted: That Messrs. Welcome Arnold and Richard
          Salter have an order on Stephen Hopkins Esq.
          for the sum of one thousand dollars, they
          paying the cash to the treasury in month. (bill
          signed)

Voted: That Messrs. Ambrose Page, Joseph and Wil-
          liam Russell, and Nicholas Brown have an
          order on Stephen Hopkins Esq. for two thou-
          sand eight hundred and fifty dollars. (order
          granted)

Reckoning: [   ]

          Meeting adjourned to Monday evening.

****
Monday evening March 11, 1776

Meeting in being according to adjournment.

Present: Honble. Nicholas Cooke Esq.
Nicholas Brown
Daniel Tillinghast
Joseph Brown
Joseph Nightingale
John I. Clark
Jabez Bowen

Voted: That Messrs. Clark and Nightingale have an order on Stephen Hopkins Esq. for two thousand five hundred dollars on the said Stephen Hopkins Esq. (order granted)

Voted: That Nicholas and John Brown have an order on Stephen Hopkins Esq. for two thousand four hundred dollars (order granted)

Voted: That the secretary make out an order to send to Mr. Francis Lewis, merchant, New York, and desire him to ship the two hundred bolts of duck purchased of him by Stephen Hopkins Esq. by the *Diana*, Jonathan Carpenter, master, for this place.

Reckoning: [ ]

Meeting adjourned to Wednesday evening.
****

Wednesday evening March 13, 1776

Meeting in being according to adjournment.

Present: Honble. Nicholas Cooke Esq.
Nicholas Brown
Daniel Tillinghast
Joseph Brown
John Brown

Joseph Nightingale
John I. Clark
William Russell
Jabez Bowen

Voted: That Zephaniah Andrews'[17] account amounting to ten pound seven shillings 7d be paid Mr.
George Olney. (order granted)

Reckoning: [   ]

Meeting adjourned to Friday evening.
****

Friday evening March 15, 1776
Meeting in being according to adjournment.

Present: Honble. Nicholas Cooke Esq.
Nicholas Brown
John Brown
Joseph Brown
Daniel Tillinghast
Joseph Nightingale
John I. Clark
William Russell
Jabez Bowen

Voted: That the balance of Cromwell Child's account
amounting to the sum of [   ] be paid out of the
committee treasury.

Voted: That Messrs. Rotch and Jarvis have an order
on Stephen Hopkins Esq. for one thousand
dollars, and that the same be paid the treasurer
on his delivering the bills. (order granted)

Voted: That the pumps for the large ship be made 20
feet long and for the smallest, 19 feet.

Reckoning: [   ]

Meeting adjourned to Monday evening.
****

Monday evening March 18, 1776

Meeting in being according to adjournment.

Present: Nicholas Brown
Joseph Russell
John Brown
Joseph Nightingale
William Russell
Joseph Brown
Daniel Tillinghast

Voted: That Mr. John Brown have an order [on] Stephen Hopkins Esq. for two thousand five hundred dollars, and that he account with treasury for the same.

Reckoning: [ ]

Meeting adjourned to Wednesday evening.

****

Wednesday evening March 20, 1776

Meeting in being according to adjournment.

Present: Nicholas Brown
Joseph Russell
William Russell
John Brown
Joseph Nightingale
Jabez Bowen

Voted: That Daniel Tillinghast's account amounting to forty-two pounds twelve shillings and eleven pence be paid him out of the committee's treasury.

Whereas this committee have purchased a considerable quantity of spars more than will be wanted for the ships now building here, it is voted that they be sold to any persons that may want the same after the ships are supplied, at the following prices, via., for all spars under 8inches, at one shilling per inch; for top masts etc. above 8 inches and not exceeding 10 inches, at 1/6 per inch; for booms and bowsprits, as they may be for length and bigness, from five to ten dollars per piece; for masts from 12 to 20 inches diameter to be from 6 to 9 shillings per inch.

Reckoning: [ ]

Meeting adjourned to Friday evening.

****

Friday evening March 22, 1776

Meeting in being according to adjournment.

Present: Nicholas Brown
Joseph Brown
John Brown
Daniel Tillinghast
Joseph Nightingale
William Russell
Jabez Bowen

Reckoning: [ ]

Meeting adjourned to Monday evening.

****

Monday evening March 25, 1776

Meeting in being according to adjournment.

Present: Honble. Nicholas Cooke Esq.
Nicholas Brown
Joseph Russell
John Smith
Joseph Nightingale
John I. Clark

William Russell
John Brown
Jabez Bowen
Whereas there seems to be an uneasiness among the ship carpenters on account of their wages, 'tis voted that Nicholas Cooke Esq., John Smith, William Russell, and Jabez Bowen be a committee to attend in the yard tomorrow morning to settle the matter with them, they not allowing any one carpenter more than 9d more than they were to have in the former agreement.

Reckoning: [   ]

Meeting adjourned to tomorrow evening.
****
Tuesday evening March 26, 1776

Meeting in being according to adjournment.

Present: Honble. Nicholas Cooke Esq.
            Nicholas Brown
            Daniel Tillinghast
            Joseph Brown
            Joseph Nightingale
            Henry Ward
            John I. Clark
            Jabez Bowen

Voted: That Mr. E. Palmer get the masts and yards that he has procured for the ships rafted from Taunton down to Mount Hope on the best terms he can, and that he give the committee intelligence as soon as he gets them to Swansea.

Voted: That the balance of Mr. Elkanah Palmer's account be paid him by the treasurer.

Reckoning: [   ]

Meeting adjourned to Friday evening.
****

Friday evening March 29, 1776

Present: Nicholas Brown
Joseph Russell
Joseph Brown
John Brown
Daniel Tillinghast
Joseph Nightingale
William Russell
Jabez Bowen

Voted: That the sum of thirty-six pounds lawful money be paid Mr. Joshua Hacker for forty-five water casks for the ships. (order granted)

Reckoning: [   ]

Meeting adjourned to Tuesday evening.
****

Wednesday evening April 10, 1776

Meeting in being according to adjournment.

Present: Honble. Nicholas Cooke Esq.
Nicholas Brown
Joseph Brown
William Russell
Joseph Russell
John Smith
Henry Ward
John I. Clark
Jabez Bowen

Voted: That fifty pounds lawful money be paid to Mr. John Manley by the treasurer.
Meeting adjourned to Friday evening.
****

Friday evening April 12, 1776

Meeting in being according to adjournment.

Present: Honble. Nicholas Cooke Esq.
Nicholas Brown
Joseph Russell
John Brown
Henry Ward
John I. Clark
Jabez Bowen

Voted: That the sum of one thousand and eighty-five pounds four shillings and ten pence be paid Messrs. Clark and Nightingale, being the balance of their account, out of the treasury.
That seventy-two pounds be paid Nicholas Cooke Esq. for twelve bolts of duck bought of Jacob Greene.[18] That seven pounds be paid Nicholas Cooke Esq., being the amount of his account.
That nine pounds twelve shillings and eight pence be paid James Marsh, being the amount of his account. That seven pounds one shilling be paid Elisha Brown[19] out of the treasury, being the amount of his account.

Voted: That one hundred and sixty cutlasses be purchased of Benjamin Comstock @ 9/- per piece.
Meeting adjourned to Monday evening.
****

Monday evening April 15, 1776

Meeting in being according to adjournment.

Present: Honble. Nicholas Cooke Esq.
Nicholas Brown
Joseph Brown

Joseph Russell
John Brown
Joseph Nightingale
John I. Clark
Jabez Bowen

Voted: That there be an examination among the calk-
ers, and that a subcommittee with a master
calker of each ship fix the prices that each one
shall have, and that the boys' wages be particularly considered and settled, that Mr. John
Brown be the committee.

Voted: That the assistants that work with the head
riggers that are not particularly agreed with
have not more than 4/6 per day for their work.

Voted: That this committee agree to take all the Rav-
en's-duck that Messrs. Clark and Nightingale
and Captain Joseph Cooke[20] have to sell @ 14
dollars per piece, suppose one hundred bolts.
Meeting adjourned to Friday evening.
****

Friday evening and Monday evening the committee met but did no business of importance
and adjourned to Wednesday evening.
****

Wednesday evening April 24, 1776

Meeting in being according to adjournment.

Present: Nicholas Brown
Henry Ward
Joseph Nightingale
John I. Clark
William Russell
Daniel Tillinghast
Jabez Bowen

Voted: That the sum of six pounds three shillings and

four pounds two shillings and eight pence be paid Mr. Charles Jenckes out of the treasury. (order granted) Meeting adjourned to Friday evening.

****

Friday evening April 26, 1776

Meeting in being according to adjournment.

Present: Honble. Nicholas Cooke Esq.
           Nicholas Brown
           Henry Ward
           Daniel Tillinghast
           Joseph Nightingale
           John I. Clark
           William Russell
           John Smith
           Jabez Bowen

Voted: That five pounds fifteen shillings and three pence be paid Samuel Coy for painting, out of the treasury. (order granted)

Voted: That one pound ten shillings and nine pence be paid John Smith out of the treasury for expenses in sending to Hingham for ship carpenters.

Voted: That forty firearms be purchased of Captain Joseph Cooke for the use of the ships at three pounds L My per piece.

Voted: That Captain Christopher Sheldon procure two good and faithful men to watch the ships till they are launched to prevent accidents etc.

Voted: That seven pounds three shillings and six pence L My be paid Elisha Mowry Esq., being the balance of his account, for timber.

Meeting adjourned to Monday evening.

****

Monday evening April 30, 1776

Meeting in being according to adjournment.

Present: Honble. Nicholas Cooke Esq.
Nicholas Brown
Joseph Brown
Joseph Russell
William Russell
John Brown
John I. Clark
Joseph Nightingale
Daniel Tillinghast

Voted: That twelve eighteen pounders be made for the large ship and only six eighteen pounders for the small ship, and that the quarterdeck and forecastle guns be six pounders, and that the whole six, twelve, and eighteen pounders be all fifteen diameters of the ball.

Voted: That Richard Marvin be appointed third lieutenant of one of the Continental ships building here. He is assigned to the largest ship.

****

Wednesday evening May 15, 1776

Meeting in being according to adjournment.

Present: Honble. Nicholas Cooke Esq.
Henry Ward
Joseph Brown
John Brown
Daniel Tillinghast
Joseph Nightingale
William Russell
John Smith
Jabez Bowen

Whereas Major Benjamin Tallman has safely launched the ship that he was building and it is determined that the other ship may be launched on Saturday, provided that Major Tallman gets the ways up, it is thereupon voted that the sum of fifty dollars be paid to the master builders of each yard to be expended in providing an entertainment for the carpenters that worked on the ships.

Voted: That one third of the sum of the agreement made with Captain Pendleton be paid him for the disappointment he met with in not bringing the provisions from New Haven bought there for the fleet.

Voted: That the committee's treasurer pay the sum of twelve hundred dollars to Esek Hopkins Esq.[21] for a bill drawn by him on the Continental treasurers at Philadelphia.

****

Monday evening May 20, 1776

Meeting in being according to adjournment.

Present: Joseph Brown
Daniel Tillinghast
William Russell
Jabez Bowen

Voted: That Mr. John Manley have an order on the treasury [of] fifty pounds lawful money. (granted)

Voted: That the sum of one hundred pounds sixteen shillings and six pence L My be paid Mr. William Giles out of the treasury as per order from Mr. John Manley and charge the same to Mr. Manley's account.

****

Wednesday evening May 22, 1776

Meeting in being according to adjournment.
Present: Nicholas Brown Esq.
Joseph Russell
John Smith
William Russell
Jabez Bowen
Captain William Barron[22] of Newport having
produced sufficient testimonials of his seaman-
ship and other qualifications, he is appointed
master of the largest of the ships and is desired
to attend on board as soon as may be.
****
Friday evening May 24, 1776

Meeting in being according to adjournment.
Present: Nicholas Brown
Joseph Brown
Daniel Tillinghast
John Smith
Jabez Bowen
Voted: That two hundred and thirty-six pounds six
shillings and eight pence L My be paid Messrs.
Nathanael Greene and Company out of the
treasury. (order granted)
Voted: That the sum of eighty-five pounds five shil-
lings and six pence be paid Mr. Joseph Brown
for 3T. 3C. OH, 18 2/3pd. bar iron at £27 per
ton out of the treasury.
****
Monday evening May 27, 1776

Meeting in being according to adjournment.
Present: Nicholas Brown

Joseph Brown
Daniel Tillinghast
John Smith
Jabez Bowen
Joseph Russell
Henry Ward
Joseph Nightingale
William Russell

Voted: That Captain John [B.] Hopkins[23] write a letter to Captain Adamson of Boston offering him to be first lieutenant of one of the ships building here and desire his answer as soon as may be, or if Captain Hopkins is well enough to go to Boston to transact this business, the committee will defray his expenses, if Captain Hopkins declines writing, that Col. Bowen write him as recommended to the Col. by Admiral [Esek] Hopkins.

Voted: That Mr. James Eldred of South Kinston be appointed a midshipman for one of the new ships.

Voted: That the sum of eight pounds five shillings be paid Mr. Joshua Hacker for 26 water casks. (order granted)

Voted: That the sum of fourteen pounds sixteen shillings and nine pence be paid Mr. Nathaniel Gilmore out of the treasury for blacksmith's work done for the ships' boats. (O. G.)

****

Wednesday evening May 29, 1776

Meeting in being according to adjournment.

Present: Nicholas Brown
Joseph Russell
Joseph Brown

Daniel Tillinghast
Joseph Nightingale
William Russell
Jabez Bowen

Voted: That Mr. Samuel Shaw of Bridgewater be appointed a midshipman on board the largest ship.

Voted: That Mr. William Jennison of Mendon be appointed first lieutenant of marines for one of the new ships of war fitting here, on his enlisting twenty-five good men in one month from this date, that shall pass muster by the committee.

Voted: That Henry Ward Esq. get two hundred of the Continental Congress invitations to the seamen printed on the most reasonable terms he can immediately.

****

Friday evening May 31, 1776

Meeting in being according to adjournment.

Present: Nicholas Brown
Henry Ward
John Smith
Joseph Brown
William Russell
Daniel Tillinghast
Jabez Bowen

Voted: That the balance of Mr. Francis Brindley's account be paid out of the treasury, provided the quantity charged has been received, on examining the clerks' books.

Voted: That Captain James Sellers of Dartmouth be appointed third lieutenant of one of the ships of war fitting here, on his enlisting 12 good seamen to go in the ships within 20 days.

Voted: That all the rigging that Messrs. Brindley and Maudsley have to spare be engaged for the ships at 16 dollars per hundred.

****

Wednesday evening June 5, 1776

Meeting in being according to adjournment.

Present: Nicholas Brown
Joseph Russell
Daniel Tillinghast
William Russell
Joseph Nightingale
Jabez Bowen

Voted: That sixty pounds L My be paid Mr. William Jennison, lieutenant of marines, in order to enlist his complement of men, on his procuring sufficient sureties.

****

Friday evening June 7, 1776

Meeting in being according to adjournment.

Present: Honble. Nicholas Cooke Esq.
Henry Ward
Nicholas Brown
Daniel Tillinghast
Joseph Nightingale
John I. Clark
Joseph Brown
Jabez Bowen

Voted: That the sum of thirty-three pounds fourteen shillings and three pence be paid to Captain Pardon Sheldon out of the treasury. (O. G.)

Voted: That the sum of fifty-eight pounds eight shillings and ten pence be paid Stephen and Gideon Jenckes out of the treasury. (O. G.)

****

Wednesday evening June 12, 1776

Meeting in being according to adjournment.

Present: Nicholas Brown
Joseph Brown
Joseph Nightingale
Daniel Tillinghast
John I. Clark
Jabez Bowen

Voted: That eighty pounds L My be paid Mr. John Manley out of the treasury to pay for cordage etc.

Voted: That six pounds be paid Mr. Richard Marvin out of the treasury for one month's wages. (O. G.)

****

Friday evening June 14, 1776

Meeting in being according to adjournment.

Present: Joseph Russell
Joseph Brown
Daniel Tillinghast
John I. Clark
Nicholas Brown

Voted: That the ship joiners be allowed five shillings L My per day from this date.

Voted: That Mr. Paul Hathaway be appointed 3rd mate of one of the ships, provided he enlists 6 seamen, the men to be got in 10 days.

Voted: That John Grannis be Captain George Stillman's first lieutenant and Barnabas Lothrop, second lieutenant of marines on board the ship *Warren*.

****

June 20, 1776

Present: Nicholas Cooke Esq.
Henry Ward
Nicholas Brown
Joseph Brown
John Brown
Joseph Nightingale
Joseph Russell
Jabez Bowen

Voted: That a captain of marines shall enlist forty good men; a 1st lieutenant, thirty-three; a second lieutenant, twenty-seven, before they be entitled to their commissions. That Silas Davol (of Tiverton) be appointed captain of marines to the ship *Providence*.
That Mr. William Barron be appointed first lieutenant of the ship *Providence*.
That James Sellers be second lieutenant of the ship *Warren*. That Benjamin Page be third lieutenant of the ship *Providence*.
That Niles Christian be second mate of the ship *Warren*.

****

June 24, 1776

Voted: That Seth Chapin be second lieutenant of marines for the ship *Providence*.
That twenty barrels of flour be delivered Charles Bower to bake into ship bread.

****

June 26, 1776

Voted: That Lemuel Carver be appointed a midshipman on board the ship *Warren*.
That Ebenezer Allen (of Rochester) be appointed steward of the ship *Warren*.

****

June 28. Voted that there be two iron hearths
procured for the ships, also that there be four
iron cabooses sent for to New York.

Voted: That the blacksmiths that engaged to do the
work for the *Warren* be desired to meet the
committee tomorrow morning, 9 o'clock, on
board the said ship, that they may determine
who should do the work that is yet necessary to
be done.

****

July 6 voted that we exchange the pork now at
New Haven belonging to the ships for the like
quantity to be received of Robert Smith.

Voted: That Avery Parker be appointed first lieutenant of marines on board the *PROVIDENCE* on
his enlisting thirty-three good men in twenty
days from this date.

Voted: That William Dunton, William Comstock, and
Thomas Bowen be appointed midshipmen, the
two first on board the *Warren* and Bowen on
board the *Providence*.

****

June 8. Voted that Mr. John Brown pay such
sums of money as he shall think necessary to
the recruiting officers from time to time, and
that the treasurer supply him accordingly.

Voted: That Mr. William Barron be appointed to pay

the board of the people that belong to the ship *Providence*.

Voted: That Messrs. John Brown, John Smith, and William Russell be appointed a committee to settle the treasurer's accounts, likewise Mr. George Olney's accounts.

Voted: That the sum of six hundred pounds lawful money be paid Rufus Hopkins Esq.[24] in part for the cannon making for the ships.

Voted: That Niles Christian be appointed chief mate on board the *Warren* if he signs the articles tomorrow morning.

Voted: That John Channing be appointed second lieutenant of the ship *Providence*.

As there is not a sufficiency of medicines to be procured in New England,

Voted: That Jabez Bowen write to Stephen Hopkins Esq. requesting him to procure an order from the Marine Committee for Dr. Morgan to put up two medicine chests with the necessary instruments for the two ships of war fitting here, and that the same be forwarded here as soon as possible.

Voted: That Simeon Dunbar be appointed a midshipman on board the *Warren*.

Voted: That there be three hundred swivel shot delivered Mr. Pain for the use of the vessel that he is going to Charlestown in, he being employed by that government to transport a number of seamen in the service of that state hither, on his paying 3d per piece for the 8 oz. and 2d per piece for the 6 oz. shot.

Voted: That Nicholas Easton Gardiner be appointed a midshipman on board the ship *Providence*.

Voted: That Samuel Knapp be chief cook of the
          Warren.
Present: at the above meeting
          Nicholas Brown, chairman
          Joseph Russell
          Joseph Brown
          John Brown
          Joseph Nightingale
          Daniel Tillinghast
          Henry Ward
          William Russell
          Jabez Bowen
                  ****
                                             July 24, 1776

Present: Nicholas Cooke Esq.
          Nicholas Brown
          John Brown
          Henry Ward
          Joseph Nightingale
          William Russell
          Daniel Tillinghast
          Jabez Bowen
Voted: That a bill be drawn on the Honble. Stephen
          Hopkins Esq. at Philadelphia for eight hun-
          dred and forty dollars in favor of Mr. Peter T.
          Curtenius of New York.
Voted: That Benjamin Eddy build a new barge and a
          skiff for the ship *Warren* under the direction of
          Captain John B. Hopkins.
Voted: That Mr. Jonathan Ellis be paid forty pounds
          lawful money out of the treasury in part of his
          hand bill and for boxing blocks.

Voted: That Mr. Joseph Burrough[25] and the other people at the state's laboratory be employed to procure and put up the gunners' stores for both the ships of war.

****

August 3, 1776

Whereas we have had the misfortune in heaving out the ship *Warren* this day to carry away her foremast and to spring her mainmast, which must greatly retard the completing the said ship etc, but that we may do all in our powers to have them replaced, 'tis voted that Col. William Russell go to Middletown and there procure one mainmast to work 28 inches, 87 feet long, one foremast 27 inches diameter, 80 feet long, one mizzenmast 26 inches diameter, 78 feet long, also spars for main and topsail yards and topmasts, and that a vessel be procured to bring them around here on the best terms they can and as soon as possible. If spars are to be got, the vessel is to be loaded with them.

Voted: That Mr. Daniel Hawkins go to Portsmouth and there procure masts and spars of the above dimensions, that he hire a vessel on the best terms he can and freight the spars here, taking smaller ones enough to load her, that he spare no reasonable expense in dispatching this business as soon as he can, and that the treasurer supply him with money.

Voted: That Jabez Bowen write letters to Mr. Barnabas Deane[26] of Weathersfield, [Connecticut], and John Langdon Esq. of Portsmouth, [New Hampshire], to procure the above spars for this committee.

Voted: That Messrs. Russell be desired to write to Mr. William Foster and request him to purchase two hundred butts for water casks for the ships and have them transported here as soon as possible.

Voted: That there be a bill drawn on the Honble. Stephen Hopkins Esq. (at Philadelphia) for one thousand dollars in favor of Mr. Welcome Arnold, he paying the cash here in one month.

Voted: That Mr. James Sumner[28] be paid ten shillings per day for his and his boys' wages from last Monday morning, provided he keeps steadily to work till he has finished the gun carriages, also that [   ] Cord be allowed five shillings per day from this date, provided he continues to work with Mr. Sumner.

****

August 23

Voted: That Mr. John Smith be desired to go to Cumberland and contract with Jeremiah Wilkinson for sticks for the cheeks for the masts, and that he procure them cut and carted as soon as possible, and that Mr. Benjamin Tallman go with him to forward the work.

Voted: That six shillings per day be paid to John Lindsey and the other persons that work on the gun carriages with Mr. Sumner.

Voted: That [   ] Tanner be appointed a midshipman and Benjamin Dunham second mate on board the *Providence*.

Voted: That Mr. Barron, lieutenant of the *Providence*, desired to go to Newbury and Portsmouth and examine the ships of war building there, and that he report what improvements he finds in them, that his expenses be paid him.

Voted: That Mr. John Brown be requested to write to New York and purchase ten tons of cordage for the ships, and that it be shipped here as soon as may be.

Voted: That the commanding officer of the *Providence* order thirty tons of pig iron on board the said ship, and that a suitable number of casks be filled with water and put on board, and that all dispatch be made to get her below as soon as possible.

****

August 29

Voted: That the sum of one hundred and six pounds twelve shillings and six pence 3/4 be paid Mr. John Smith out of the treasury as the balance of his account. 'Tis agreed to pay Captain Christopher Sheldon six pounds lawful money for the damage done his wharf in launching the ships.

****

September 2

Voted: That sixty-nine pounds twelve shillings L My be paid Deacon Timothy Newell for the amount of his bill, and that Jabez Bowen remit the same to him.

Voted: That a letter be written to the Navy Board at Philadelphia recommending Abraham Whip-

ple Esq.[29] (now of the *Columbus*) to be appointed captain of the ship *Providence*, and that
Messrs. William Russell and Jabez Bowen write
by the next post.

****

September 6, 1776

Meeting in being.

Present: Honble. Nicholas Cooke Esq.
           Nicholas Brown
           Joseph Russell
           Henry Ward
           Joseph Brown
           William Russell
           Joseph Nightingale
           John I. Clark
           John Smith
           John Brown
           Jabez Bowen

John Langdon Esq., the agent appointed to
build and equip a ship of war at Portsmouth
for the thirteen United States, applied to this
committee to send him twenty-six twelve and
six six pounders, and he procuring a paper
from the Honble. Stephen Hopkins recommending to the owners of the Furnace Hope to
supply him with the said guns if they had so
many made, and Esek Hopkins Esq., commander in chief of the American Navy, being
present, recommended to the committee also
that they should spare the guns, etc., whereup-
on this committee voted to supply Mr. Langdon with the guns, provided he makes a contract with the owners of the furnace to replace

those that he takes as soon as possible, which we suppose will not exceed fifty days, provided they are supplied with water by the falling of the Fall rains.

****

September 14, 1776

Meeting in being etc.

Voted: That the committee purchase of Messrs. Clark and Nightingale one thirteen inch cable of one hundred and twenty fathoms at five pounds L My per C inch.

Voted: That Mr. Shaw go to the Eastern Furnaces and engage a quantity of shot for the ships, and that Mr. Joseph Brown be desired to give him the quantity and dimensions of those that are wanted.

Voted: That Captain Christopher Sheldon be appointed to pay off the board of the seamen and marines belonging to the two ships, and that his wages be raised to one dollar per day for his attendance etc.

Voted: That Mr. George Olney be not retained any longer in the pay of the committee, he having nearly posted up the books etc etc.

****

September 23, 1776

Meeting convened.

Present: Honble. Stephen Hopkins and several of the committee.

Voted: That the ships be equipped with all expedition and fitted for the sea by the 10th of October at furthest, for the effecting of which it is voted that Daniel Tillinghast Esq. be sole director for the business, that the officers apply to him for all necessaries they may stand in need of, and all the members belonging to the committee present (being nine in number) do engage to supply or procure the articles wanted according to the memorandums that shall be given out to them by Col. Tillinghast from time to time.

Voted: That the treasurer pay to Messrs. Joseph and William Russell the sum of three hundred pounds for them to remit to Mr. William Foster of Boston in part of his account.

****

September 30, 1776

Voted: That application be made to John Cole Esq.,[30] attorney at law, that he attach William Dunton's share in the privateer sloop *Montgomery's* last cruise for and in behalf of the United American States, as he belonged to the Continental fleet at the time he went the said cruise, and that all others that have left the service of the said ship in this harbor and have enlisted on board privateers, that they be served in like manner.

Voted: That Captain Christopher Sheldon pay Mr. Jonathan Ellis sixty pounds L My in part of his blacksmith's bill.

****

October 21, 1776

Meeting in being etc.
This committee having received a letter from the Marine Committee at Philadelphia in

which the conduct of this committee was much blamed for not delivering John Langdon Esq. a suite of the cannon made for the frigates built here, and as there are many things that bare hard on the characters of the committee as men, as merchants, and as gentlemen, Mr. Ward, Mr. John Brown, and Mr. Clark are appointed a committee to answer the same and forward it by the next post.

****

From the last date this committee have taken no authority on themselves to transact any new business respecting the two frigates built here, they having finished all that they thought belonged to them to do. They have accordingly delivered them to the Honble. Stephen Hopkins Esq., the person who commissioned them to build the ships. In the opinion of this committee they are fit and might proceed immediately to sea, were they fully manned. This is a matter that we have more than once mentioned to the Marine Board at Philadelphia but have had no particular directions how the men were to be obtained, so that we leave them in their care.

October 25, 1776

****

February 1777

The committee met to examine the state of the accounts and find that there is a balance of seven thousand dollars to the different tradesmen for finishing the ships. They therefore have written a letter to the Marine Board at Philadelphia requesting that the above sum of seven thousand dollars may be remitted here immediately, which letter was countersigned by Stephen Hopkins Esq., our employer, desiring the money might be sent, to which we have received no answer till July 6, in which they require all the accounts to be forwarded before the money due shall be remitted.

****

July 7, 1777

At a meeting of the committee.

Present: Honble. Nicholas Cooke Esq.
            Nicholas Brown
            Joseph Brown
            John Brown
            Daniel Tillinghast Esq.
            Jabez Bowen

This being all the members now in town. This committee having received a letter from the Honble. Marine Board at Philadelphia requesting them to forward the accounts to them that arose for building and equipping the two frigates etc. 'tis resolved that Mr. John Manley and Captain Christopher Sheldon be employed to close the accounts and make out fair copies in order to forward to Philadelphia as soon as possible.

BIOGRAPHICAL NOTES

1 Biographical sketches of the thirteen men who participated as members of the committee will be found in the appendix. Additional biographical notes have been supplied below for some of the other more prominent persons mentioned in the journal.

2 Nicholas Power was Joseph Brown's business partner at this time, as well as his father-in-law.

3 Benjamin Tallman, soon to be named the master builder for the *Warren*, was recognized as one of the foremost master ship-builders in New England. In the course of his long career he built at his India Point shipyard in Providence about one hundred merchant ships, including some of the fastest and largest of their day. After the war he built for John Brown several of the original East India traders. At the beginning of the war he joined the military as a major, quickly advancing to the rank of colonel and the command of a regiment from Rhode Island. He saw action in the Battle of Long Island. He was still involved in the military when he was summoned by the committee to return to Providence. See Edwin M. Stone, *Mechanics' Festival: An Account of the Seventy-First Anniversary of the Providence Association of Mechanics and Manufacturers* . . . , Providence, Knowles, Anthony and Co., 1860, pp. 68–69; scattered references in James B. Hedges, *The Browns of Providence Plantations, The Nineteenth Century* (vol. 2), Providence, Brown University Press, 1968, and Edward Field, *State of Rhode Island and Providence Plantations* . . . , 3 vols., Boston, Mason Publishing Col, 1902, vol. 2.

4 Christopher and Pardon Sheldon were first cousins. Both were sea captains who at one time or another were employed by the Browns (see Hedges, vol. 1 *Colonial Years*, Cambridge,

Mass., Harvard University Press, 1952, p. 27 and vol. 2, p. 30). Christopher owned the wharf area where the two frigates were built and launched.

5 This Joseph Tillinghast, probably the one who participated in the *Gaspee* incident in 1772, is either committee member Daniel's father or his cousin of the same name.

6 Joseph and Daniel Bucklin were first cousins in the blacksmith business together. Joseph became involved early in revolutionary agitation and participated in the Gaspee incident in 1772. See Field, vol. 1 pp. 461–463; William R. Staples, *Annals of the Town of Providence* . . . , Providence, Knowles and Vose, 1843, scattered references.

7 Sylvester Bowers, soon to be named master builder for the *Providence*, must have been an expert shipwright to be capable of drawing up plans for the two frigates. He began his career as a ship carpenter in Somerset, Massachusetts. About 1750 he established himself as a shipwright at Pawtucket, where he remained in business for many years (see Field, vol. 2, p. 400).

8 This John Manley would appear to be a Newport resident and not the John Manley who commanded a makeshift fleet under General Washington's orders during 1776 off the Massachusetts coast and who subsequently commanded the *Hancock*, one of the new frigates built at Newburyport. See Charles Oscar Paullin, *The Navy of the American Revolution* . . . , Chicago, Burrows Brothers Co., 1906, pp. 64–69; William James Morgan, *Captains to the Northward, the New England Captains in the Continental Navy*, Barre, Mass., Barre Gazette, 1959, scattered references.

9 Nicholas Cooke, Jr., was the son of Nicholas Cooke, the committee member. He was twenty-two years old in 1776. Joseph Dolbear Russell was the son of Joseph Russell, the Committee member. He was then twenty years old.

10 Stephen Hopkins (1707–1785), as Rhode Island representative to the Continental Congress, was the most influential

public figure in the colony at the time. He had been chairman of the old Naval Committee, which had commissioned the first American naval fleet (originally only four refitted merchant ships) under the command of his brother Esek. Then, as a member of the expanded and renamed Marine Committee, he was responsible for overseeing the Rhode Island segment of the Continental frigate-building project. To handle these matters directly in Providence, he had appointed the committee of thirteen members. Now the committee had to go through him to receive operating funds.

Hopkins was a merchant by trade, but the greater part of his adult life was spent in public service. By the 1730s he was active in Scituate town politics and was representing his home district in the General Assembly. He also began to assume judicial duties, which by 1747 earned him a seat on the Superior Court. Between 1754 and 1768 he fought an annual running battle with Samuel Ward of Westerly (who in 1774–1776 joined him as representative to the Continental Congress) for the Rhode Island governorship. Hopkins managed to win more often than Ward (ten out of fourteen years). In the early 1770s he became chief justice of the Superior Court and again served in the General Assembly until he went to Philadelphia. Through the years he also found time to be the first chancellor of the College of Rhode Island, helped found the *Providence Gazette* in 1762, and was an ardent and vocal supporter of colonial union and revolutionary patriotism for many years before the war. In 1772, as chief justice, he insured that the instigators of the *Gaspee* incident were never tried.

During the Stamp Act crisis Hopkins wrote *The Rights of Colonies Examined*, a widely acclaimed work that has recently been republished by the Rhode Island Bicentennial Commission. He is also credited with persuading Rhode Island authorities to be the first to issue calls to the other colonies for both the Stamp Act Congress of 1765 and the Continental Congress in 1774.

In September 1776, after signing the Declaration of Indepen-

dence with William Ellery for Rhode Island, Hopkins re-
turned to Providence in ill health. This did not stop him from
serving again in the General Assembly, however, and he
remained a prominent figure until his death. See William E.
Foster, *Stephen Hopkins, a Rhode Island Statesman* . . . , 2 vols.,
Providence, S. J. Rider, 1884; the *Dictionary of American
Biography*; *Biographical Cyclopedia of Representative Men of
Rhode Island*, Providence, National Biographical Publishing
Co., 1881, p. 99; scattered references in Paullin, Morgan, and
Field.

11   This is probably the George Olney who spent most of the war
as General Nathanael Greene's private secretary. After the
war he was for many years town treasurer of Providence (see *A
Geneology of the Descendants of Thomas Olney*, compiled by James
H. Olney, Providence, Freeman and Son, 1889, p. 32).

12   Welcome Arnold was one of Providence's leading merchants
and public figures. He was not chosen to serve on the
committee, but he apparently profited from the project in any
case.

13   William Ellery (1727–1820) was a prominent Newport merchant and public figure whose small contribution to the
building of the two frigates was shortly to be overshadowed by
events of greater import. When Samuel Ward died on March
25, 1776, just over a month after the date of this journal entry,
Ellery was chosen to fill his seat at the Continental Congress.
Thus, he joined Stephen Hopkins in signing the Declaration
of Independence for Rhode Island. He remained in the
Continental Congress until 1786, except for two years when
he lost the elections. In 1779 he was appointed to the Board of
Admiralty, which replaced the Marine Committee. From 1786
to 1790 he served as commissioner of the Continental Loan
Office at Newport. From 1790 until his death he served as
federal collector of customs at Newport. See the *Dictionary of
American Biography* and the *Biographical Cyclopedia*, pp. 99–100.

14   This is probably Welcome Arnold's younger brother.

15   Hezekiah Sabin of Killingly, Connecticut, was a merchant in

New Haven. His daughter, Hannah, married Nicholas Cooke in 1740. In 1800–1801 either Hezekiah or his son, Hezekiah Jr., worked as manager of John Brown's distillery while the latter was serving in the U. S. Congress (see Hedges, vol. 2, p. 13).

16 Nathanael Greene and Company was the family iron-forging business at Potowomut (Warwick), Rhode Island, founded by the father of Nathanael Greene, the Continental Army general. In 1779 the family business was prospering sufficiently to expand to a second site on the Pawtuxet River in Coventry. Nathanael Sr. was a staunch Quaker; thus Nathanael Jr.'s military exploits were not admired at home. After the war the famous but debt-ridden general retired to a plantation on the Savannah River in Georgia, where in 1786 he died of sunstroke. See the *Dictionary of American Biography*; the *Biographical Cyclopedia*, pp. 15–16; *Representative Men and Old Families of Rhode Island*, Chicago, J. H. Beers & Co., 1908, pp. 1250–1251; Field, scattered references.

17 Zephaniah Andrews was a prominent mason in Providence who worked on such important buildings as John Brown's house, Joseph Russell's house, and University Hall. He was wealthy enough to be involved in matters of high public and private finance with the leading merchants of Providence. See *Mechanics' Festival*, pp. 113–114; scattered references in Staples.

18 Jacob Greene was the brother of General Nathanael Greene.

19 This Elisha Brown is probably the uncle of the famous brothers. He was born in 1717 and died in 1802.

20 This Joseph Cooke is probably the son of Nicholas Cooke. He was thirty years old in 1776.

21 Esek Hopkins (1718–1802), then commodore of the first American naval fleet, probably needed this money for supplies for his fleet, which at the time was holed up at Providence after completing with limited success its first cruise. He had a

reputation for unorthodox dealings, but apparently both he and the committee felt sure that his brother Stephen Hopkins would handle any fiscal irregularities. In August 1776 Esek was officially censured by the Marine Committee for disobeying orders on the fleet's first cruise (by sending the fleet to New Providence instead of cruising the southern American coast) and for failing to capture the British ship *Glasgow* off Newport despite its being alone against his eight-ship fleet. He continually failed to please Congress, so that in June 1777 he was suspended and by January 1778 was dismissed outright. During that whole period the fleet, including the new frigates, had failed to make a major foray since the New Providence expedition. He was unpopular with Congress, which was partly due to his own tendency to disregard orders if they seemed improper to him, and also apparently the result of a strong southern sectional prejudice against (and jealousy of ?) the New England commodore. He continued to be a prominent figure in Rhode Island public life after his dismissal. See the *Dictionary of American Biography*; *Biographical Cyclopedia*, pp. 19–20; scattered references in Field, Morgan, and Paullin; Edward Field, *Esek Hopkins, Commander-in-Chief of the Continental Navy* . . . , Providence, Preston & Rounds, 1898.

22 Though William Barron was originally named sailing-master of *Warren*, he was given considerable responsibility by the committee and was soon appointed first lieutenant on the frigate *Providence*. In 1778 he was first lieutenant on the frigate *Boston* off the English coast when he lost his life accidentally after a cannon burst near him (see Morgan, pp. 132–133).

23 John Burroughs Hopkins, the eldest son of Commodore Esek Hopkins, had been appointed to be one of the four original ship captains of the Continental Navy, commanding the *Cabot* under his father. During the engagement with the *Glasgow* on the fleet's homeward voyage, the *Cabot*, which was the most directly involved, received much fire, and her captain was among the wounded. At the time of this journal entry, John was still recovering from his wound, which accounts for the

question in the committee's mind about whether he was well enough to go to Boston. John did recover in time to be named captain of the *Warren*. After relatively successful service for two years, he, like his father, came under a cloud in Congress. In 1779 he was investigated, then suspended. This patriot, who had participated in the *Gaspee* incident in 1772, was not ready to give up, however. He spent the rest of the war as a privateer captain. After the war he lived an obscure private life until he died in 1796. See the *Dictionary of American Biography*; scattered references in Field, Morgan, and Paullin.

24 Rufus Hopkins was appointed to be a member of the committee by his father, Stephen Hopkins. He had not attended a meeting, however, since January 29. The Hope Furnace, of which he was the manager and part owner with the Brown brothers, supplied cannon throughout the American colonies for the war effort. See biographical sketch of Rufus Hopkins in the Appendix.

25 John Burrough was a well-known scientist in Providence. On June 3, 1769, he observed the "transit of Venus" with such other scientifically inclined persons as Joseph Brown, Stephen Hopkins, Moses Brown, Jabez Bowen, Benjamin West, and Joseph Nash (see Staples, p. 619).

26 Barnabas Deane had been appointed by his brother Silas (member of the original Naval Committee and of the Marine Committee) to direct construction of the frigate *Trumbull* at Chatham, Connecticut (see Morgan, p. 65).

27 John Langdon, a member of the Naval Committee, but no longer a representative to the Continental Congress in 1776, was appointed by Josiah Bartlett, New Hampshire's representative on the Marine Committee, to take charge of the construction of the frigate *Raleigh* at Portsmouth (see Morgan, p. 67).

28 James Sumner was a "master workman" who came from Boston to Providence in 1775 to supervise some of the

construction of the First Baptist Meeting House (see Norman Isham, *The Meeting House of the First Baptist Church in Providence: A History of the Fabric*, Providence, 1925, p. 11).

29 Abraham Whipple started his career as a merchant sea captain under the Nicholas Brown firm. During the French and Indian War he was a privateer captain. In 1761 he married Sarah Hopkins, sister of Stephen and Esek Hopkins. He was a prominent participant in the *Gaspee* incident in 1772. In Esek Hopkins' first fleet, he commanded the *Columbus* on the New Providence expedition. For a short time before that, he had commanded the sloop *Katy*, renamed *Providence*, which he had sailed to Philadelphia. In the days of congressional displeasure following the New Providence expedition, he requested and received a court-martial, which declared him innocent of cowardice but guilty of errors in judgment. Given this verdict and his close association with the ill-fated Esek Hopkins, it is interesting that the committee's request to name him captain of the frigate *Providence* was subsequently honored. He went on to a successful naval career until, in 1780, he and the *Providence* were captured as Charleston fell to the British. Instead of executing him as the British had promised to do after the *Gaspee* incident, they paroled him to Chester, Pennsylvania, where he stayed until the war ended. After the war he returned to a farm in Cranston but soon moved to Marietta, Ohio. In 1801 he sailed on one of the few square-rigged ships built on the Ohio River on a commercial voyage via New Orleans to Havana and Philadelphia. See the *Dictionary of American Biography*; *Biographical Cyclopedia*, pp. 117–118; scattered references in Field, Morgan, and Paullin.

30 John Cole led a long and distinguished career as attorney and judge. He also served in the General Assembly from 1762 to 1775. He was involved early in the revolutionary cause, carrying word to Boston of Rhode Island's support of Massachusetts' stand against the Stamp Act and serving with Stephen Hopkins, Moses Brown, Henry Ward and others on the colony's first committee of correspondence, among other things. In 1775 he became the advocate general for the Rhode Island Maritime or Vice-Admiralty Court, a position he held

until his death in 1777. In this capacity he was the proper official to approach concerning this novel case of naval-privateer legal conflict (see *Biographical Cyclopedia*, pp. 115–116; Field, vol. 1, p. 223n; Staples, p. 657).

BIOGRAPHICAL SKETCHES OF THE COMMITTEE MEMBERS

The following biographical sketches flesh out the lives of the thirteen (eleven of whom were active) members of the committee. The most interesting observations about the members as a group concern their close business ties as merchants (and thus their joint economic interest in the shipbuilding project), their closely intertwined social, political, and marital ties, and their deep involvement, simultaneous with their shipbuilding efforts for the Navy, in privateering ventures which throughout the war competed directly with the fledgling Navy for shipyard space, shipbuilding labor and materials, crewmen, and prizes.

NICHOLAS COOKE (1717–1782) was performing the duties of the first governor of the state of Rhode Island (1776–1778) when he was appointed to the Committee. He was a native of Providence, the son of Daniel and Mary (Power) Cooke. Early in life he became successfully engaged in the sea trade, first as a ship captain, then as a wealthy merchant. He used his wealth to expand his enterprises into manufacturing (especially ropemaking and distilling) and invested extensively in land. In 1740 he married Hannah Sabin of Killingly, Connecticut (whose father and brother both profited in the ship building project). By the 1750s he was actively involved with friends like Stephen Hopkins in revolutionary agitation. During the Revolution he mixed principle and profit in extensive privateering activities. He joined other public-minded merchants in supporting the growth of higher education as a trustee of the College of Rhode Island (opened in 1767 in Warren, moved to Providence in 1770, renamed Brown University in 1804). In 1775 he was elected deputy governor of Rhode Island colony. When revolutionary hostilities broke out, Governor Wanton of Newport, a pacifist, resigned, leaving Cooke to be acting governor. Cooke remained in office as Rhode Island declared itself a state. Cooke was chosen by the committee to be its chairman.

NICHOLAS BROWN (1729–1791) was the oldest of the four famous sons of James and Hope (Power) Brown of Providence. Before the revolutionary conflict he led the brothers, through the firm of Nicholas Brown and Company, in the establishment of a mercantile and manufacturing empire. Though the brothers gradually split up after 1771 until the firm was disbanded in 1774, they retained joint ownership of the spermaceti candle factory and Hope Furnace. Nicholas also continued in the mercantile business, occasionally trading jointly with his brothers John and Joseph. He was active in privateering throughout the Revolutionary War. After the war he joined with George Benson, who had been a clerk with the old Nicholas Brown firm, to establish the new firm of Brown and Benson. As a prominent businessman, he also became involved in educational development and politics. He was an early and steady supporter of the College of Rhode Island. In the 1750s he served as a representative to the General Assembly. From 1766 to 1772 he served in the Providence Town Council. He was also an active member and benefactor of the Baptist Society. His first wife was the daughter of Providence judge and merchant Daniel Jenckes. Nicholas' high status in the Providence business community made him a logical choice to be the committee's treasurer and paymaster.

JOSEPH BROWN (1733–1785) was the second oldest of the famous four sons of James and Hope (Power) Brown of Providence. He participated in the activities of the family firm, Nicholas Brown and Company, primarily as manager of the spermaceti candle factory, but he never deeply committed himself to business enterprise. His interests were more intellectual, scientific, and creative. Thus he did play a key role in the establishment of the Hope Furnace and was enthusiastic later in helping convert it for war production. Soon after the firm disbanded in 1774, he joined with Nicholas Power in the new firm of Brown and Power. It did not greatly prosper, however. Joseph's real interest was science. In 1784 he took on the chair in experimental philosophy at the College of Rhode Island, a position which he held until his death and which earned him membership in the American Academy of Sciences. His most visible and lasting contributions to Providence were made as an amateur architect. Buildings which he designed or

helped design include University Hall (the original 1770 building
of the College of Rhode Island, constructed by Nicholas Brown
and Company), the Town Market House (construction in 1773
directed by Joseph Brown and Stephen Hopkins), a house for his
own family (1774), the First Baptist Meeting House (1774), a house
for his brother John Brown (1786), and a house for Joseph Russell
on North Main Street. As a prominent citizen, Joseph also became
involved in politics, serving in the General Assembly in 1775, when
he worked with Esek Hopkins to strengthen local defenses, and
again in the early 1780s. In 1759 Joseph married Elizabeth,
daughter of Nicholas Power, subsequently his business partner
(and to whom he was related through his mother). He was an active
Freemason and a devout Baptist.

JOHN BROWN (1736–1803) was the third of the four famous
sons of James and Hope (Power) Brown of Providence. The most
independently energetic and enterprising of the brothers, in 1771
he was the first to drop out of the family firm. He was an aggressive
merchant, intent upon increasing his profits without much regard
to moral or legal limits. Thus he developed an extensive slave
trade, defending it on the basis of its profits. He also was a leader in
the conspiracy to burn the British revenue schooner *Gaspee* in
1772. During the Revolution he was a staunch patriot, actively
involved in privateering. After the war he pioneered direct trading
with the East Indies and China starting in the late 1780s. He soon
joined with his son-in-law, John Francis, to establish the new firm
of Brown and Francis, which greatly expanded the East India
trade. John was an early supporter of education. In 1767 he
contributed with Jabez Bowen and others to an attempt (which
failed) to establish a free public school in Providence. He also
supported the College of Rhode Island, serving as college treasurer
from 1775 to 1796. From 1776 through 1787 John was an off-and-
on representative to the General Assembly. He was elected to the
Continental Congress in 1784 and 1785. In 1787 he strongly
supported the U. S. Constitution. In 1799 he was elected a U. S.
representative for one term. In 1760 he married Sarah, daughter
of Daniel Smith (a relative of John Smith). He was active in the
Baptist Society and contributed to the building of the First Baptist
Meeting House in 1775. He also constructed a large mansion for
himself, designed by his brother Joseph.

JOSEPH RUSSELL (1732–1792), the son of Thomas Russell of Providence, was a prominent merchant in partnership with his brother William. Their firm prospered for thirty years primarily in trade with England and the West Indies. During the Revolution the firm was involved in privateering. After the War the brothers also went into the whaling business. Joseph was also a prominent public figure in Providence. He was a trustee of the College of Rhode Island, an active member of the Episcopal Church, and a leading Freemason. His second of three wives was Amey Smith, a step-daughter of Stephen Hopkins. Late in life Joseph retired to Woodstock, Connecticut, where he died.

WILLIAM RUSSELL (1739–1825), the son of Thomas Russell of Providence, was a prominent merchant for thirty years in partnership with his brother Joseph. Like his brother, he was a trustee of the College of Rhode Island. Unlike his brother, he participated directly in the Revolutionary military effort, though only at home as a colonel in the defense-oriented Providence Cadets. He never married.

JABEZ BOWEN (1739–1815), the son of Ephraim and Mary Bowen of Providence, was a leading merchant and intellectual figure. He graduated from Yale in 1757. His early success in the mercantile trade, including privateering during the Revolution, left him free to engage in a variety of public activities. In the same year he returned from Yale, he helped found St. John's Lodge of Freemasonry in Providence, and he went on to hold prominent positions in that lodge and in the Rhode Island Grand Lodge, founded in 1791. In 1767 he contributed with John Brown and others to an attempt (which failed) to establish a free public school in Providence. Also in 1767 he helped found the College of Rhode Island, and he served on its Board of Fellows from 1768 to 1785, was briefly a trustee, then was chosen chancellor, a position he held for thirty years until his death. He served on the Providence Town Council from 1773 to 1775, in the General Assembly in 1777 and 1788–1790, as deputy governor from 1778 to 1780, and as judge of the Superior Court for many years. In 1790, as a delegate to the state's constitutional convention, he helped assure acceptance of the U. S. Constitution by a close 34-32 vote. During Washington's presidency he served in the appointive position of commissioner of loans in Rhode Island. His first of two marriages was to Sarah, the daughter of Obadiah Brown. His intellectual background made him the logical second choice of the committee to be secretary after it was learned that Henry Ward was too busy to attend and perform the secretarial duties.

JOHN INNES CLARK (1745–1808) was a prominent merchant in Providence in partnership with Joseph Nightingale. Both Clark, separately, and the firm of Clark and Nightingale were involved in privateering during the Revolution. Following the lead of John Brown, the partners invested deeply after 1787 in the East India trade. In 1775 Clark was made a major in the First Providence Regiment of militia. Though he saw no action, he did help plan military strategy in the city's Council of War in 1780 and was on the committee to wait on the visiting French commanders in 1780. In 1779 he briefly held office as a representative to the General Assembly. He married Lydia Bowen (probably the stepsister of Jabez Bowen) in 1773. After it was found that Nicholas Brown was too busy to perform the duties of treasurer and paymaster for the committee, Clark was elected to take his place.

JOSEPH NIGHTINGALE (1748–1797) was the son of Samuel Nightingale. He was a partner with John Innes Clark in the firm of Clark and Nightingale. Like his partner, Nightingale was involved in a variety of public activities. In 1774 he served on a commission to revise the militia laws. During the war he was a captain and later a colonel in the Providence Cadets. After the war, in 1784 and again in 1787, he served as a representative to the General Assembly. In 1769 he married Elizabeth, the daughter of Captain George Corlis.

JOHN SMITH (1734–1817) was the son of Captain William Smith of Providence. In 1756 he was an officer on a privateer. Soon he became a merchant of importance, apparently in partnership with his stepfather, William Smith. He also became a large landholder in Providence. He was part owner during the Revolution of several privateers, including one named *Montgomery*. He was a trustee of the College of Rhode Island. He served for many years in the General Assembly. During the Revolutionary War he served on the

Commission of War. He also was active in the Episcopal Church and probably in Freemasonry. His wife was Eliphal Arnold of Newport. Late in life he moved to a farm in Johnston, Rhode Island, where he spent his last years.

DANIEL TILLINGHAST (1732–1806), the son of Joseph Tillinghast of Providence, was a merchant of some wealth. He was involved early with the colonial militia, commanding an artillery company in 1763. He attained the rank of colonel. Perhaps because he operated no privateers of his own during the Revolution, he was appointed by Congress in 1776 to be Rhode Island's Continental prize agent. Beyond his prize duties, he was given broad responsibilities to oversee other marine functions of the Continental Congress. Thus on September 23, near the end of the Committee's deliberations, the Committee (with Stephen Hopkins in attendance), gave him full responsibility for the day-to-day supervision of the project. These appointments and responsibilities are interesting, since Tillinghast was not prominent in public offices and other activities as were most other committee members. Nepotism was certainly on his side, for in 1763 he had married Lydia, daughter of Stephen Hopkins. After the war he became involved with John Brown in the merchant and distilling businesses. He was an active Freemason for many years.

HENRY WARD (1732–1797) is a lesser-known member of a famous Newport family. His father Richard and his brother Samuel were both governors of the colony of Rhode Island. Samuel was for many years archrival of Stephen Hopkins for that office, though the two made up just in time to work together in Philadelphia (1774–1776) representing Rhode Island in both Continental Congresses. Samuel died just weeks short of the signing of the Declaration of Independence and was replaced by William Ellery. Henry was well educated but apparently not a strong public leader. He spent the bulk of his adult life in the single post of secretary, first of the colony, then the state of Rhode Island from 1760 to 1797. He succeeded Samuel in this position. He was the natural choice of the committee to be its secretary, but apparently his duties to the state made him too busy to take on this task. He was soon replaced by Jabez Bowen.

RUFUS HOPKINS (1727–1813) was the eldest son of Stephen and Sarah Hopkins. Early in life he went to sea, becoming a ship's commander. In 1766 he joined the Brown brothers, becoming manager of the new Hope Furnace. He remained in this position, becoming through the years a part owner, for most of the rest of his life, though he apparently was a merchant on the side. In 1806 the Browns withdrew from the furnace operation, and it was purchased by Rufus' son Sylvanus and associates. Rufus was involved in many public activities. He was a trustee of the College of Rhode Island from 1782 until his death; he represented Scituate for many years in the General Assembly; he was a judge of the Court of Common Pleas for Providence County and briefly a justice of the Superior Court. The influence of the Hopkins family in early naval history is worth noting. Stephen Hopkins, Rufus' father, as representative to the Continental Congress and member of the Marine Committee, appointed the committee to build the two ships. Esek Hopkins, Stephen's brother, was the first commodore of the Navy. John Burroughs Hopkins, Esek's eldest son, was one of the original ship commanders in the Navy. Also, two other committee members (Joseph Russell and Daniel Tillinghast) were married to relatives of Stephen Hopkins. Rufus did not actively participate in the activities of the commitee. According to the journal, he attended only three meetings, all in January.

SOURCES OF BIOGRAPHICAL INFORMATION

A. *General Sources*

Biographical Cyclopedia of Representative Men of Rhode Island, Providence, National Biographical Publishing Co., 1881.

Field, Edward, *State of Rhode Island and Providence Plantations* . . . , 3 vols., Boston, Mason Publishing Co., 1902.

Hedges, James B., *The Browns of Providence Plantations*, vol. 1, Cambridge, Mass., Harvard University Press, 1952, vol. 2, Providence, Brown University Press, 1968.

Representative Men and Old Families of Rhode Island, Chicago, J. H. Beers & Co., 1908.

Staples, William R. *Annals of the Town of Providence* . . . , Providence, Knowles and Vose, 1843.

B. *Specific Sources*

Chad Browne Memorial . . . , compiled by a descendant, Brooklyn, N. Y., printed for the family, 1888.

"Clarke" Families of Rhode Island . . . , compiled by George Austin Morrison, Jr., New York, Press of the Evening Post Job Printing House [1902].

Correspondence of Governor Samuel Ward . . . and Genealogy of the Ward Family . . . , compiled by Clifford P. Monahon, Providence, Rhode Island Historical Society, 1952.

Farnham, Charles William, "John Smith, the Miller, of Providence, Rhode Island, Some of His Descendants", *Rhode Island History*, 1961–1965, vols. 20–24.

Genealogy of One Line of the Hopkins Family, compiled by a descendant, Providence, J. A. and R. A. Reid, 1881.

"Genealogy of the Nightingale Family", compiled by William Waterman Chapin, Providence, 1912, typescript in library of the RIHS.

Genealogy of . . . the Russell Family, compiled by John Russell Bartlett, Providence, privately printed, 1879.

"Tillinghast Genealogy", compiled by William R. Tillinghast, 2 vols., [Providence], 1944, typescript in the library of the RIHS.

APPENDIX

JOURNAL OF THE RHODE ISLAND GENERAL ASSEMBLY[1]
[Providence, Saturday, August 26, 1775]

Whereas notwithstanding the humble and dutiful petition of the last Congress to the King, and other wise pacific measures taken for obtaining a happy reconciliation between Great Britain and the Colonies; the ministry, lost to every sentiment of justice, liberty and humanity, continue to send troops and ships of war into America, which destroy our trade, plunder and burn our towns, and murder the good people of these colonies,—

It is therefore voted and resolved, that this Colony most ardently wish to see the former friendship, harmony and intercourse, between Great Britain and these Colonies restored, and a happy and lasting connection established between both countries, upon terms of just and equal liberty; and will concur with the other colonies in all proper measures for obtaining those desirable blessings; and as every principle divine and human require us to obey that great and fundamental law of nature, self preservation, until peace shall be restored upon constitutional principles; this colony will most-heartily exert the whole power of government, in conjunction with the other colonies, for carrying on this just and necessary war, and bringing the same to a happy issue. And amongst other measures for obtaining this most desirable purpose, this Assembly is persuaded, that the building and equipping an American fleet, as soon as possible, would greatly and essentially conduce to the preservation of the lives, liberty and property of the good people of these Colonies and therefore instruct their delegates to use their whole influence at the ensuing congress for building at the Continental expenses a fleet of sufficient force, for the protection of these colonies, and for employing them in such

1. Bartlett, ed., *Records of Rhode Island*, VII, pp. 368–374.

manner and places as will most effectually annoy our enemies, and contribute to the common defence of these colonies, and they are also instructed to use all their influence for carrying on the war in the most vigorous manner, until peace, liberty and safety, are restored and secured to these Colonies upon an equitable and permanent basis.

It is voted and resolved, that the monthly wages of Abraham Whipple, captain of the colony sloop, be raised from £ 7.10s. to £ 9, from the time he entered on board said sloop.

JOHN ADAMS TO JAMES WARREN[1]

[Philadelphia], Octr. 19, 1775

Dr. Sir,—What Think you of an American Fleet? I don't Mean 100 ships of the Line, by a Fleet, but I suppose this Term may be applied to any naval Force consisting of several Vessells, tho the Number, the Weight of Metal, or the Quantity of Tonnage may be small.

The Expence would be very great—true. But the Expence might be born and perhaps the Profits and Benefits to be obtained by it, would be a Compensation. A naval Force might be created which would do something. It would destroy Single Cutters and Cruisers. It might destroy small Corvets or Fleets of these like [Sir James] Wallace's at R. Island and Ld. Dunmores at Virginia. It might oblige our Enemies to sail in Fleets. For two or three Vessells of 36 and twenty Guns, well armed and manned might attack and carry a 64 or a 70 or a 50 Gun Ship.

But, there is a great Objection to this. All the Trade of Pennsylvania, the Lower Counties, a great Part of Maryland and N. Jersey Sails in between the Capes of Delaware Bay. And if a strong Fleet should be posted in that Bay, Superiour to our Fleet it might obstruct all the Trade of this River.

Further the Trade of Virginia and the rest of Maryland floats

1. *Warren-Adams Letters* . . ., vol. 1, 1743–1777, Massachusetts Historical Society, *Collections*, vol. 72, 1917, pp. 145–146.

into Chesapeake Bay between the Capes of Henry and Charles where a Fleet might stop all. Besides Virginia and Maryland have no Navigation of their own nor any Carpenters to build ships. Their whole Trade is carried on in British Bottoms by British, most of it by North British Merchants. These Circumstances distinguish them quite from New England, where the Inlets are innumerable and the Navigation all their own.

They agree that a Fleet, would protect and secure the Trade of New England but deny that it would that of the Southern Colonies.

Will it not be difficult to persuade them then to bear the Expense of building a Fleet, merely for N. England. We are Speculating now about Things at a Distance. Should we be driven to a War at all Points, a Fleet a public Fleet as well as privateers might make prey enough of the Trade of our Enemies to make it worth while.

[No signature.]

VOTE OF THE CONTINENTAL MARINE COMMITTEE[1]

[Copy]   Marine Committee Decr 16, 1775
Agreed   That the Thirty two Gun ships be of the following Dimensions Vizt

The Gun Deck 132 feet 1 Inch
    Keel   110 Do 10 3/4 Inches
    Beam   34 Do 5 1/2 Inches
    Hold   11 feet

That the 24 Gun Ships be of the Same dimensions as the *Hero* Privateer built in the City of Philadelphia in the Last War—the[n] follows the *Hero's* Dimensions[2]

1. Captain J. G. M. Stone Private Collection, Annapolis. This copy was made for John Langdon, who was to build one of the thirty-two gun frigates in Portsmouth, New Hampshire, and, as he was not interested in the smaller ships, the dimensions for them were omitted from his copy.
2. The *Hero* was built at Philadelphia in 1762 by James Penrose. Her principal dimensions were 120 feet 6 inches by 95 feet 6 inches by 32 feet 6 inches by 10 feet 6 inches. Marion V. Brewington, "The Designs of Our First Frigates," *The American Neptune*, VIII, No. 1, January 1948, p. 16.

BENJAMIN TALLMAN TO THE RHODE ISLAND GENERAL COMMITTEE[1]

To the Hon'ble the General Committee appointed to act during the Recess of the General Assembly.
May it please your Honors
Having been urged in the most pressing Manner by the Naval Committee to undertake the Building of One of the Frigates ordered to be built in this Town, and having given my Consent thereto from Motives of the publick Interest without any Desire to quit the Service of my Country in that Department in which I at present am Engaged I desire leave to resign my Commission as Major of a Regiment in the Rhode Island Troops and to be discharged: I am Your Honor's [&c.]
Providence Jany 25th 1776   Benjᵃ Tallman

1. Council of War Papers, RIHS.

ADVERTISEMENT OF THE RHODE ISLAND NAVAL COMMITTEE[1]

The Naval Committee having received Orders to appoint the Officers for the two Ships of War building here, take this Method to request all Gentlemen, who are desirous to engage in that Service, to send in their Names, with their Recommendations, to some of the Committee, as soon as may be.
All able-bodied Seamen, that are willing to serve on board said Ship, may apply as above; and they shall be entered into immediate Pay.
Providence, May 9, 1776

1. _Providence Gazette_, May 11, 1776.

WILLIAM ELLERY TO GOVERNOR NICHOLAS COOKE[1]

[Extract]   Philadelphia June 21st 1776
John [Burroughs] Hopkins is appointed to the Command of the largest Ship, called _Warren_ after Dr. [Joseph] Warren of glorious

Memory, and Samuel Tompkins to the Command of the smallest called *Providence*.—[2]

1. "Revolutionary Correspondence of Governor Nicholas Cooke," *Proceedings of the American Antiquarian Society, New Series*, XXXVI, pp. 326, 327.
2. Command of *Providence* actually went to Abraham Whipple.

CONTRACT FOR CONSTRUCTION OF
TWO CONTINENTAL FRIGATES AT NEWBURYPORT[1]

Articles of Agreement made this First day of March 1776. Between The Honble Thomas Cushing Esqr of Dedham, on the one part, and Jonathn Greenleaf, Stephen Cross, and Ralph Cross of Newbury port shipwrights on the Other part.

Wittneseth, That the Said Jonathan Stephen & Ralph hath agreed with the Said Thomas to build with the utmost dispatch in Newbury port Afforesaid two Ships for the Account of The Thirteen United Colonies. Agreeable to the Draughts & Directions which the Said Thomas hath Deliver'd them, viz. The Length of the keel of the one Ship, About Ninety Six feet, Bredth of Beam About Thirty three feet Depth in the Hold about Ten feet Six Inches. Between decks about four feet Six Inches the Waist five feet:[2] The Length of the keel of the other Ship About one hundred & eleven feet Bredth of Beam about thirty five feet, depth in the Hold about Eleven feet, depth Between Decks about five feet, & five feet waist,[3] the Said Ships to be built as near as possible to the draughts & directions Above mentioned & Referr'd to, And the timber and plank to be of the best white Oak, and free of Rots and defects except in the bottom where they have Liberty to put some black Oak timber only, And the decks which are to be Laid with good pine plank the scantlens of timber and thickness of plank to be agreeable to the Directions Above Referr'd to, To find and make a Compleat Set of Masts Yards Bowsprit, Topmasts and top gallant mast the main and fore mast of each ship to be Cheek'd with Oak in a good and workmanlike manner, to build a head & Galleries to each Ship, to find and make two Capstons to each Ship, to fix & Step two pumps which work by hand in each Ship, to find and fix a Sufficient number of Belaying Bitts, To find and fix Suitable pillars to all the Beams above and Below. To find and fix a Rudder and Tiller to each Ship, to find & fix five Anchor Stocks for each ship. To find Sufficient stuff for the Companions, & All the gangway and other Ladders. To Caulk the ships. To find & fix all the Stocks for the Swivel guns. To find & Fix Seven pair standards between decks, and pointers over the transoms abaft in a word to do and find all the Carpenters work in the finishing them off as a Ship of War Ought to be finished, in a good and Workmanlike manner, And to Launch Said Ships Safely a float the Small ship in May the Large ship in June 1776 And the said Jonathan, Stephen & Ralph Agree Allso to Stop all the Worm holes to Clear the timbers and hold of all the Chips, to pay both Ships with Turpentine to Grave both Ships After Launching, to Water both ships on the Stocks, to find Rum for the Labourers, and to Launch Said Ships at their own Risque and Expence. And the Said Thomas Cushing Esqr on his part doth also Agree with the Said Jonathan Stephen & Ralph, that he will find for building the two Ships aforesaid and in Season, Iron work of every kind, pitch Tar, turpentine, Oackum, Joiners Work, proper tackles to assist them and all such Articles as are Customary for the owners to find and do, And pay to the Said Jonathan, Stephen & Ralph at the Rate of Six pounds ten shills L Money p tun for each and every tun the Large ship shall measure And Six pounds of Like money for each & every tun the smaller Ship may measure the payments to be made in the following manner viz one fourth part when the keel is Laid, one fourth when shut in under the Whale one fourth when the Gun Deck Beams are Carried in one eighth part when Launch'd the Remaining Eight part when finished. To the true and faithfull performance of each and every Article before mentioned, the parties bind and oblige themselves each to the Other in the penal sum of Two Thousand pounds Law money. In Wittness whereof we have hereunto interchangably set our hands and Seals the day & year first above written

Signed Sealed & deliverd   Jonath Greenleaf
   in presence of   Step[n] Cross
John Bradford   Ralph Cross [Junr]
Gibbins Sharp   Thomas Cushing

1. US Naval Academy Museum.
2. Subsequently the Continental frigate *Boston*.
3. Subsequently the Continental frigate *Hancock*.

Account of Medicines Supplied to the Continental Frigates by the
Greenleaf Apothecary Shop, Boston.

the United American States Dr.

1777					
Jany. 23d	To a Chest of Medicines for the Continental Frigate Boston	272	£119	1	4
April 1st.	To a Chest of Medicines for the Continental Frigate Hancock	286	£156	14	11
May 13	To sundry Medicines for the Continental Frigate Boston		4	11	—
			£280	7	3
28	To a Chest of Medicines for the Continental Frigate Providence		135	0	8
	To Sundry Medicines for the Continental Frigate Columbus		79	12	6
			£214	13	2

INDEX

ABOUT THE AUTHOR

JOHN FITZHUGH MILLAR received his A.B. from Harvard in 1966 and his M.A. in History from the College of William & Mary in 1981. He has taught history at three colleges and spent a decade as a museum director in Rhode Island. He has devoted years to the study of various aspects of life in the seventeenth and eighteenth centuries, such as architecture, decorative arts, classical & folk music, dance, ships and military history, and has lectured extensively on these subjects (anyone interested in hiring Mr. Millar to give lectures is invited to write to him in care of Thirteen Colonies Press). He has gained practical experience with eighteenth-century ships (including under sail) by arranging for the construction and operation of full-sized copies of the 24-gun frigate *Rose* (1757/1970) and the 12-gun sloop *Providence* (1768/1976). He served for many years on the Rhode Island Bicentennial Commission and in 1970 he founded the Bicentennial Council of the Thirteen Original States, an organization that successfully raised millions of dollars to assist Bicentennial projects in the Thirteen States. He lives with his wife Cathy in Williamsburg, Virginia.

His major published works include:

A HANDBOOK ON THE FOUNDING OF AUSTRALIA 1788
CLASSICAL ARCHITECTURE IN RENAISSANCE EUROPE 1419–1585, 1987
EARLY AMERICAN SHIPS, 1986
ELIZABETHAN COUNTRY DANCES, 1986
A COMPLETE LIFE OF CHRIST, 1986
AMERICAN SHIPS OF THE COLONIAL & REVOLUTIONARY PERIODS, 1978
SHIPS OF THE AMERICAN REVOLUTION, 1976
RHODE ISLAND: FORGOTTEN LEADER OF THE REVOLUTIONARY ERA, 1975
COLONIAL & REVOLUTIONARY WAR SEA SONGS & CHANTEYS, 1975
THE ARCHITECTS OF THE AMERICAN COLONIES, 1968

Thirteen Colonies Press

710 SOUTH HENRY STREET, WILLIAMSBURG, VIRGINIA, 23185-4113

804-229-1775

EARLY AMERICAN SHIPS

VALOUR FORE & AFT The story of the
sloop *Providence* 1775 - 1779

CLASSICAL ARCHITECTURE IN RENAISSANCE
EUROPE 1419-1585

HARRISON: *New England Colonial Designs by*
Peter Harrison (1716-1775)

ELIZABETHAN COUNTRY DANCES

COUNTRY DANCES OF COLONIAL AMERICA

EARLY AMERICAN BAROQUE &
CLASSICAL MUSIC

A COMPLETE LIFE OF CHRIST

A HANDBOOK ON THE FOUNDING OF
AUSTRALIA 1788

RHODE ISLAND: FORGOTTEN LEADER OF
THE REVOLUTIONARY ERA